ADVANCED PRAISE FOR GOD LOVES ME, I THINK...

Buckle up for a bumpy ride over spiritual terrain that some might consider taboo. *God Loves Me, I Think* is a hilarious and gritty journey across staunchly held religious beliefs, secrets, traumas, and the Lone Star state in search of unconditional peace. Sure, we all know about unconditional love, but does God grant peace with no strings attached? Stacey Robbins is a masterful storyteller who leads the way, ending up in a surprising new awareness of what it means to know God and trust in Him. For anyone with questions for God, or about Him, *God Loves Me, I Think* can help guide you to your inner truth and a deeper understanding of spiritual peace.

Tracy Panzarella
Author, Screenwriter, and Lifestyle Host at KOLO and KRNV News

If you've ever longed to believe that God loves you but have struggled with deeply rooted narratives that appear to provide evidence to the contrary, *God Loves Me, I Think* is for you. With abject honesty, Stacey lays it all out on the table in this chronicle of faith and doubt in which limiting beliefs unravel bit by bit to reveal the heart-healing love of God. Far from a dry spiritual diary, *God Loves Me...I Think* is a hilarious, insightful, inspiring trek through turmoil to peace, through pain to healing, and through fear to love.

Lisa Espinoza
Speaker, Certified Grief and Loss Counselor, and Author of First, Brush Your Teeth — Grief and Loss in Real Time

The way Stacey describes her connection with God makes more sense to me than any sermon I've ever heard. This is a book about healing, genuine connection, and the sacred power of rest — some of the most meaningful themes of the times. Her vulnerability and honesty moved me as much as her beautiful storytelling abilities. The story of her spiritual growth and how she found grace could not have come at a more poignant moment in my own spiritual journey. The wisdom she found and generously shares with us in *God Loves Me, I Think* is a genuine gift.

Lori Beth Auldridge
Creator & Host of Elevating Motherhood Podcast

Exasperated by rules and regulations she'd been taught were conditional to earning God's love, a crisis of faith and quest for inner peace unfolds in this captivatingly-entertaining journey with author Stacey Robbins.

In her pursuit, Stacey faces moments of self-examination that most aren't brave enough or willing to share. Her queries into how she can trust a God often depicted as relishing in punishment are laid bare and ultimately lead her through the difficult process of learning what it means to be still…to "hear" God speak His truth into her life.

Stacey keeps us laughing as she openly litigates some of her life's messier moments and carves a pathway to a more peaceful existence.

Don't miss getting your hands on that recipe in this delectably-insightful book.

Irene Dunlap
Co-Author, Chicken Soup for the Soul book series
Author, TRUE: Real Stories About God Showing Up in the Lives of Teens

Tired of pretending to be someone you're not and ready for an honest look at life, love, faith, family, and a healthy dose of doubt, pain, joy, and the pursuit of peace? You've come to the right place. Stacey is a gifted communicator and storyteller who'll have you shaking your head in disbelief while simultaneously nodding in agreement. And after she invites you into her pain, she will have you laugh so loud you may snort. (Yes, I did.) I love Stacey's honesty, and her journey reminds all of us that God is with us and for us, even if we have a hard time believing that. You'll thoroughly enjoy *God Loves Me, I Think…*, and to get even more out of it, discuss it with others to explore the themes, the highs, the lows, and, yes, even that elusive peace.

Gregg Farah
Pastor and Founder of LetsMakeDisciples.org and Author of 52 Reasons to Believe

This is truly one of the most honest, self-indicting, modern writings with a willingness to evaluate oneself, and ask very hard questions about "Western Christianity" and who God really is.

Is it OK to struggle with God?
Is it OK to struggle with yourself and what you've always believed?
Is it OK to have life experiences that tell a different story than the neatly packaged narrative of Western Christianity?
Is it OK to not sweep things under the rug as though they've never existed, but to deal with them head on?
Is it OK to admit we don't have all of the answers so that we can surrender with wonder, curiosity, and continued learning which gives us the essence and power to heal?

My friend, Stacey Robbins, who is ever-fascinating and a beacon of light, has gone head-to-head with questions we all have, but are afraid to ask (and have been shamed if we do).

And because it's so 'wild', many Christians will feel challenged because we've become a religious culture that feels 'safer' when being told what we should think. But if Tozer, Spurgeon, C.S Lewis, Wesley, Whitefield, and Edwards were alive today, every single one of them would hear her out.
Are we really ready for the answers?
What if it takes us to uncomfortable places?
Are we truly willing to confront those dark places to give our lives permission to heal, grow and learn?

I'm in. *Are you?*
Let's journey together with Stacey in her new book, *God Loves Me, I Think... Stories from Hell, Heaven and the Other Side of Texas.*
Ken Tamplin
Music Artist, Film Composer, International Vocal Instructor

You hold in your hands a New York Times Best Seller, but people just don't know it yet. No matter your spiritual background or stage of life, you'll quickly find yourself laughing at Stacey's topsy-turvy stories, drinking in her practical wisdom, and feeling her loving embrace through every word on the page. If life has been a bumpy ride for you and you wonder if you're loved, this book is the healing heart-opener you've been longing for... and your friends will thank you for giving them a copy!
David Trotter
Business Growth Consultant and Author of Empowered to Rise

Also by Stacey Robbins

An Unconventional Life: Where Messes and Magic Collide

You're Not Crazy and You're Not Alone: Losing the Victim, Finding Your Sense of Humor, and Learning to Love Yourself through Hashimoto's

Bloom Beautiful

GOD LOVES ME

Stories from Hell, Heaven,
and the Other Side of Texas

I Think...

STACEY ROBBINS

God Loves Me, I Think… Stories from Hell, Heaven, and the Other Side of Texas

First printing, 2022

ISBN: 978-1-935798-18-7

Stacey Robbins
427 East 17th Street Box 123
Costa Mesa, CA 92627
www.staceyrobbins.com

Disclaimer: This book is intended to be an inspiring companion to your inner spiritual journey, offering encouragement and empowerment to the reader. This book is not intended as a substitute for psychological treatment or the advice of a mental health professional. This book IS intended to affirm you as you thoughtfully consider the paradigms of your spiritual beliefs and the paths it takes you; you are not alone, and you are allowed to ask questions and re-examine everything in this pursuit of wholeness and peace.

Cover / Interior Design and Photos: David Trotter

Scriptures taken from the Holy Bible, New International Version®, NIV®. Copyright © 1973, 1978, 1984, 2011 by Biblica, Inc.™ Used by permission of Zondervan. All rights reserved worldwide. www.zondervan.com The "NIV" and "New International Version" are trademarks registered in the United States Patent and Trademark Office by Biblica, Inc.™

To Caleb and Seth:

I had a vision when I was about 14 years-old of walking through a
wild brush.
With a machete and my hands, I struggled through blindly, and
step-by-step, eventually I cleared it.
When I got to the end, with scrapes all over my arms, and sweat
beading down my face,
I turned around and saw I had made a path.

Now, knowing you and how beautiful, generous, and
uncomplicated your spirituality is
– and how healing your lives are –
I see how important it is
to have done this big work of the heart.

This book, and my life journey, is dedicated to you, the families
that will one day come through you, and every life you touch.

I love you so much.
Enjoy your freedom.

It was worth it.

Dear Seeker of Peace,

You are so brave.
Yes, **you.**

You, who are shaking in your spiritual boots and afraid of doing this whole thing 'wrong.'
You, who have a million questions for God, or maybe just one, big, strong one.
You, who are risking a lot to even open up these pages, but you just can't stop yourself.

You
Are
SO
Brave.

I remember when my friend, Lyndia, spoke those words to me, "Stacey, you are so brave. To ask questions. To take the spiritual path that you did… that was very brave of you."

I looked at her like she had a squirrel sitting on her head.

I didn't understand how she could see me that way when I had actually felt foolish and afraid – weak and indulgent – and extremely and profoundly lost during so much of the process.

It took me a long time to see myself as anything but a mess.

You see, there's a lot of pressure on women in the Christian world to do our spiritual journey 'right'.
Like there's a right way and a wrong way.
Well, actually, like there's **one** *right way and a scrillion wrong ways.*

Many ways to mess up and one, small, needle-in-a-haystack 'right' way to deal with our questions, doubts, and fears.

So, we look around at each other in the church basement, over biscuits and gravy, peach cobbler, and Jell-o salad – and we wonder, "Does she think about these things too in the middle of the night? Do her questions keep her awake and restless, or is it just me?"

Because how can I say I believe in a God of Peace but I'm so anxious?
A God of Joy but I'm so down?
A God of Love, but I'm so afraid?

We look for faded smiles or weary sighs, or a prescription of Xanax peeking out of the edge of a purse – anything to let us know that maybe we're not alone.

We don't want to blow our good-girl cover because the risks are no small deal either.

Things like:

Pissing off God.
Putting our self and loved ones at risk of being punished in some way.
Going to Hell.

Not to mention, losing our family, our friends, and our credibility.
Maybe even our jobs and our ministry.

Because asking spiritual questions isn't seen as something benign like,

"Hey, could you pass the ketchup..."

Or, "Where do you want to go on vacation this summer?"

Nope. There's this whole idea around asking questions that can make people in your circle wonder about you and your faith. That can make it feel like you're under a microscope while you're trying to ask hard and honest questions.

There's a lot to lose.

So, to surrender the ideas of doing it 'right'
And to risk all the consequences of doing it 'wrong'
So that we could do it 'real'
And live in an honest place of peace...

Asking questions that rise to the surface of our God-relationship
Instead of squashing them down with good works and weak smiles...

Instead of settling for the private chronic, spiritual anxiety and public social acceptance...

Is incredibly
And sincerely

Brave.

I can't give you an award for doing this hard thing,
but I can give you my story
so that you don't feel so alone while you're living out yours.

And to remind you that you are right where you are supposed to be

And the questions have surfaced in just the right season of life,

And that this is one of the most valuable, beautiful, messy, and important spiritual times you could ever imagine.

Keep going, brave soul.

Your heart – which longs for freedom and peace... it's calling.

And this is your perfectly imperfect time to answer it.

Love,
Stacey
Seal Beach, California 2022

A Few Quick Disclaimers:

While my spiritual quest has jostled a lot of my vocabulary about all-things spiritual, I'm going to call God 'Him' for the sake of ease and continuity from where I started on this journey. I recognize there are so many ways that different cultures and different people refer to their relationship with the Divine/Source/Great Spirit. In our Western culture there's a sincere attempt to acknowledge the masculine and feminine in God but man/woman, it gets tedious to read 'He/She/It' after about half a minute. All the poetry is gone and plus, our minds can't help but smoosh words together, and 'He/She/It' starts sounding like something I'm definitely *not* going for.

Also, I'm going to make reference to hearing from God, but I've never heard God speak in some 'ghost from Scooby Doo' kind of voice. It's more a sense that I've had these voiceless words streaming through me that would show up in the oddest or most ordinary times.

That's why I tend to call God, 'Words with No Voice.' That is the way some spiritual messages are conveyed to me. Only words. No voice.

With the exception of the timeline of certain events, this story is real and true as I best remember the details in that perfectly, imperfect way that time colors, stretches, and fades as it filters through our memory. Life is also an allegory of itself, and the people who seem like villains and the people who seem like angels are really the archetypes that we all deal with in life. I'm not trying to ultimately demonize or 'angelicize' anyone. Everyone's forgiven. Everyone's appreciated. Yes. *Everyone.* The past is done, the lessons are won. I can't believe I just wrote that rhyme-y thing but I'm leaving it in there because it's true.

That's why I've changed almost all of the names and identities of people, places, and things. And the names that are not changed were allowed by permission from the brave souls who stepped lovingly beside me as I stumbled along my path — and they don't mind you knowing about it.

The timing of this story occurred when we all still had landlines and when cell phones were mostly flip phones. You could plan on losing cell service on almost all the country roads and some of the city ones depending on your carrier. Times and technology have obviously upgraded exponentially, so when the setting seems to be significantly less tech-y, you'll know why.

And there you go… I think that about covers it. You're now free to move about the cabin…

Enjoy the ride.

CONTENTS

"The greater the doubt, the greater the awakening;
The smaller the doubt, the smaller the awakening.
No doubt, no awakening."

CC Chang

*"All of humanity's problems
stem from man's inability
to sit quietly in a room alone."*

Blaise Pascal

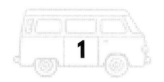

1

All in the Family

"Insanity is hereditary. You get it from your kids."

Sam Levinson

I just sat there. Staring at him. The tears of my two-and-a-half-year-old seemed to fly out of the corners of his eyes and freeze in mid-air, like he was some cartoon character come to life.

I leaned my head to the left to look at him from a different angle. Yup, he looks like a cartoon character all right – screaming with his mouth so flippin' wide you can see whatever you call that dangly thing back there.

It's 'uvula,' by the way.

I know that *now*, but I don't risk saying the medical name anymore without looking it up twice. Not since that day when I called it something that *sounded* right to me but wasn't quite sure and turned to my husband with that *"Right, honey?"* head-tilt and found him wide-eyed and speechless.

It's amazing how you can mix up a couple of letters and suddenly you're talking about the private female anatomy instead of that thing in the back of your throat.

In front of your neighbor.

Who happens to be a pastor.

My life is never boring.

"WAAAAAAA!!!"

I snapped back to the present reality where that dangly thing was in full view.

Dear Lord, where is the volume control for this child?

I plunked my elbows onto the table and put my chin down to my palms while I gazed wearily at Caleb. We had just had a *moment.* I didn't realize that my toddler was finally tall enough to reach the forbidden drawers in the kitchen until he teetered into the living room about 20 minutes earlier, proud as punch, waving some Samurai warrior steak knife up in the air like a flag.

My eyes nearly fell out of my head.

Dear Jesus…

My body focused with a surgical calm as I moved toward him, swiftly lifting the knife from his hands. With a gentle voice so he wouldn't be scared, I cooed, "Thank you for bringing this to me, sweetheart… I will move them up higher next time." He had been crying ever since losing his new 'toy,' and I was trying to remember how to breathe. The adrenaline surge that got me through that moment was quickly spiraling to a crash.

"Come here, baby." I knelt down and held out my hands as he toddled over, throwing his arms around my neck in that despairingly limp way while he screamed me deaf in my right ear. Wincing, I leaned my head as far away as I could without it detaching from my body.

That's when the home phone started ringing.

Somebody save me.

It stopped mid-ring, so Rock must have answered it upstairs. My husband was well-trained at answering a noisy phone quickly to avoid waking up any napping babies in the house.

The child in my arms was distracted by the phone for the moment. "Whaz 'at?" He became curious and then rested his head on my shoulder again as his calm, rhythmic breathing returned. In the lull, my mind drifted away: grocery lists, laundry, and life insurance were the running ticker tape in my head. Caleb breathed a big sigh as if my mental list was overwhelming him too. It brought me back to the moment we were recovering from.

"You done, honey?" I pulled back as I wiped his honey-streaked blonde bangs away from his brow and searched his deep blue eyes with the longest eyelashes I'd ever seen. "You done being sad, Cay Cay? Momma loves you sooooo much, and she can't let you play with the knives in the drawer. I'll show you how to use them when you're older. You'll understand one day."

His big eyes started tearing again as his disappointed bottom lip jutted out and started to quiver.

Oh my God. Why did I say anything? I have so much to learn in this parenting game...

He opened up again – full volume – and was so loud that I almost missed the other crying voice coming down the stairs: a tiny figure cradled in his father's arms.

Oh good. Two crying children. That's always helpful when you're on the edge.

"Sta?" Rock was calling me, but I shut my eyes tight. *You can't see me. You can't see me.* I sing-songed in my head. *It worked when I was three...*

"Stasha?" My husband tried again. "Seth's awake and very, very hungry."

Ugh. Why is someone always crying, and when is it my turn?

Sigh.

Caleb stopped crying, wiped his own tears away, and went to comfort his brother by kissing his covered toes and then toddled away to the kitchen. I turned to see my husband in a mismatched outfit of an old t-shirt that was inside out and some random swim trunks from when we were dating in the 1980s. *Ooh, now there's an interesting look.* In his arms was my blotchy-faced nine-month-old, Seth, in footy pajamas and staring intently at my chest. He snuffled and gasped, with eyebrows so red from crying that he looked like a miniature old man with a bad combover and skin condition instead of a hungry infant. He reached so far out of Rock's arms that he just about fell into mine. Meanwhile Rock ran up the stairs to get back to his phone call – and hopefully into some clothes from the 21st century.

"Hang in there, cowboy," I said to my second son, who was already so different from his big brother. While Caleb was all wide-eyed and eager, and heart on his sleeve, Seth was quiet, observing, and had an unexpected sense of humor and play – and at *that* moment was famished. I couldn't unhitch my shirt buttons fast enough, and he let out a cry of utter frustration.

"Shhh.... It's okay. It's ohhh-kaaay. We're all going to be okay..."

We're all going to be okay, right?

I'd had to talk myself down off so many ledges since having kids. With the accompanying blues of postpartum depression and being a working mom, on most days, thirty-seven felt way too old. The thyroid problems that had slammed me in my late twenties took almost all of my energy, and now, 10 years later, being an 'older mom' was siphoning off the rest.

The joys of parenting had sort of a gray sky tone over them some days, and that was hard for me to accept. I had thought that I wouldn't feel this way, and then, I felt guilty that I *shouldn't* feel this way. The guilt is consuming when you want to be more than you are for such precious, little creatures.

I loved my boys. I really did. When they weren't melting down, they were actually pretty delicious. (I licked one of them one day to see if they tasted as good as they looked. They don't, by the way. Unless you have a hankering for sweat, snot, and dried tears mixed with puréed sweet potatoes, I wouldn't recommend it.) But no matter how crazy I was about them, this parenting thing was unraveling me. Because apparently parenting required sleep. And that was the last thing my body seemed inclined to do.

And trust me, I desperately needed it because little boys are like labrador puppies — they eat, poop, run, and sleep and then repeat the pattern until they completely run out of steam. At which point it's nap time, which was *my* time to clean all the flat surfaces that I could and fret about dinner. But, despite my profound exhaustion, the moment I laid my head down at night, my mind would spin, and my body would surge like someone had plugged me into an electrical outlet.

Dear God... am I ever going to feel normal again... like I don't have tiny shards of glass in my eyes?

The heavenly glow of the young mother in a field of flowers and her child at her bosom was not my reality. Considering my body had hit its prime at 18, nursing two kids this close to 40 felt more like an extreme sport. Even so, I was from the camp of late-blooming moms (read: older) who were committed to nursing as long as we could.

My reward? My boobs were falling in direct opposite proportion to how high my dish pile was climbing. My kitchen sink looked like one of those Jenga games gone wild. Instead of washing the plates, I'd walk over with just one more to balance precariously. Holding my breath, I'd squint and wait to see if they'd all come crashing down. Thankfully, they were dirty enough to make something of a glue; floating white colonies that kept them connected to each other and had a distinctly sour odor, which I'm only slightly embarrassed to admit, I liked.

The rest of the townhouse was a nightmare. It was like Thing 1 and Thing 2 from Dr. Seuss snuck into my home in the middle of the night and threw our clothes all over the place. Only we didn't have The Cat in the Hat and that cool cleaning contraption with all the arms to straighten up afterwards.

That reminded me...

Laundry. I have to do the laundry. Why, with all the creative people in the world, hasn't anyone invented disposable clothing yet?

Sigh.

I'd be their best customer.

"Okay, Seth, other side." My voice cracked from fatigue, but he didn't notice. The big "shlurpy" suction sound that came from pulling him off made him giggle.

"Honey?" It was Rock, my brave soul of a husband trying again. He was probably checking around the corner to see if my head was spinning. Instead, he found me sitting there, wrung out at 8 a.m. with one kid under my shirt and the other in the kitchen playing drums on the pots and pans. The look on my face told him everything.

They've won.

"Oh baby..." His eyes widened as he took in the full disaster of the downstairs and me. He leaned in close so I could hear him.

"Stasha," I love that he calls me that. Just like my dad and my favorite aunt, Nancy. "I'm going to ask something, and I want you to be honest." He took a breath. "First of all, you're a great mom and a great wife, and this question has *nothing* to do with that..." I raised one eyebrow. He was negotiating a minefield and he knew it.

"I just want to know," he paused, "if it would be easier for you if I went to Target and just *bought* some more underwear..."

Ahh... that explained the swim trunk ensemble.

Waves of deep failure crashed into my already fragile psyche. I looked into his kind blue eyes. The man was a saint. He knew that me doing the laundry right now was about as likely as me building a spaceship in my spare time.

And I could tell he was concerned for my state of mind because he was talking to me in that sort of child-friendly way one talks to someone who is on the verge of a nervous breakdown.

He would have happily done the laundry himself as he was truly a household team player and had no ego about it, but I did. I insisted he leave it for me and kept assuring both of us that this day would be *the* day.

It had been five days of that, and now he wanted to know if it would be faster to *buy* new underwear instead.

One blink means yes, two blinks mean no.

I think I blinked. I needed all the help I could get right now.

Mom guilt, with some wife guilt added on.

Oh joy...

Not to mention that I looked like a wreck lately.

My roots were dark, my fingernails uneven, and the heels of my feet felt like those big squares of shredded wheat that come two to a box. I had been living in loungewear – aka sweatpants – ever since the kids were born. Apparently my sister thought I was strong enough to handle the truth. "Sta..." She stared me straight in the eyes, "I almost nominated you for What Not to Wear." Yeah, 'cause that's just what I need. Someone videotaping me while I'm bending over into the back of my SUV, trying to strap my kids into a 17-point harness car seat with sweatpants stuck up the crack of my butt.

Oh, God. When is someone going to rescue me from my life?

God.

Oh, crap. I forgot...

In the overwhelming madness of motherhood, I had agreed to go to my friend Julie's house in a few weeks to give a talk about God.

My pre-mommy career was in music. Playing piano and singing in Southern California's finest ocean-view hotels and restaurants with Rock playing the sax. Since we both shared a similar faith and wanted to serve our community, we segued to doing music in churches which eventually turned into my speaking at women's events on spiritual matters.

A term I'd come to know as 'ministry.'

Rock said I was doing ministry long before I started working at churches. We'd be shopping for eggs and milk and the next thing he would turn around and the gal at the cash register would be crying in my arms about her boyfriend leaving.

"What did you do to her?"

"Nothing." I promised. "I just asked her how she was."

After enough situations like that at the airport, local park, or pizza place, he said, "I think I figured out your secret..." he paused for effect, "You, my friend, have the gift of *Hi. How are you?*"

He added, "You're like a walking human confessional, Stace. People step into your presence and just want to tell all."

Maybe it's some kind of radar we women have with each other – we can sense when someone is safe to carry our heart with us when it feels heavy.

I wanted women to feel safe. I know what it's like to not have that, and I don't want them to feel alone. My compassion was forged because of some incredibly painful situations in my youth, only compounded by the trust issues Rock and I went through in the beginning of our young marriage. There was a myriad of experiences that I understood all too well: Keeping secrets and hiding what was really going on behind closed doors, being misunderstood by others and barely hanging on... even though I called myself a "Christian." That part was especially hard because shouldn't believing in God make your life easy and beautiful and wrapped up with a pretty bow? And even when it is messy, isn't it supposed to be Pottery Barn messy? Full of charm and style? That wasn't my life. I could make it look fine on the outside, but what was really going on was another story.

Even though I didn't share all of what was happening behind the closed doors of my home and my heart, I *was* able to share my flaws quite candidly. It comforted women to know that I could say "Christian" and "imperfect" in the same breath and that I also knew what it was like to make it through those painful situations of my youth. That my life could be messy and miraculous with some really extraordinary "God-encounters" – where He showed up in some unbelievable ways.

When you share those "Wow" moments, they make for good entertainment and inspiration, as well as a reminder that God is more involved in our lives than we imagine. That's why people would hire me from across the country to share songs and stories of encouragement and hope.

Because, there's something about hearing of a woman with a tragically hard youth, who was also told she was dying at 27, and that if she did live she'd never have kids. It made people stop in their tracks. And then, to see her standing in front of you, telling you about her broken and beautiful journey, inspires you to have hope again too.

After each event, I would sit with the women who attended – these amazing souls – and would listen to what brought them to this point of hiding their pain behind a smile. A troubled past, a teenager who won't speak to them, or a health crisis that leaves them feeling like they have to pretend that everything is okay when it's really falling apart. They were living with that mix of faith and doubt that they'd kept secret until they heard me share my story, and then they would speak in hushed whispers about what they were afraid to tell anyone else.

It wasn't just my story of reclaiming my health and finally having kids that interested women. It was my living through so much darkness and ending up with faith and a sense of humor instead of becoming a criminal. The world loves those Cinderella stories and, incidentally, so does the church.

And even though I shared openly in a way that encouraged us all, I still had this private confusion that I couldn't reconcile. I didn't understand how I could have had so many seeming *miracles* that confirmed that I was not alone and that Something Great was guiding me and yet, after re-telling my biblically epic story on the stage, I would step off and within a few hours find myself swimming in a sea of doubt again.

I guess you can have some great stories of genuine faith, but that doesn't mean you have peace.

And having peace, well..

That was what I longed for.

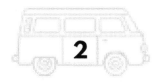

2

The Man and Me

"I love being married. It's so great to find that one special person you want to annoy for the rest of your life."

Rita Rudner

A few weeks prior to Julie's event, I had creaked softly down the stairs, holding my breath with each tiptoed step. I didn't want to wake anyone and shatter the rare silence of the morning.

Finally... could it be? A moment to myself?

I kept trying to find time alone to prepare what I was going to say to these women. Normally there was chaos from the second I woke up, but the house was quiet, and I found myself with an attention span to read something longer than the photo captions in People Magazine.

With Rock and the boys still asleep, I pulled out a book of devotions – spiritual thoughts to linger on. The words in front of me stated that The Spirit of God is evidenced by love, joy, peace, patience, and a few other things. As I continued to read, my thoughts turned to my husband. Or as I affectionately referred to him, "The Man."

The Man and I had been together since 1987 when I was 18 and he was 19. We eloped a year and half later. Oh, you can imagine our family's delight. My Italian Catholic North-East culture placed me in an extremely important position for being the first-born child of the first-born son who was also the namesake of the patriarch. As a result of that esteemed position, my wedding was supposed to be quite the shindig of the decade and not only an honor to me, but also to my father.

However, at the same moment I became engaged, my parents were going through a War of the Roses type of divorce, and it just didn't make sense to celebrate when everything between them was a battle ground. So, instead of throwing a big expensive wedding at the country club and receiving gifts in envelopes that would have provided the down payment for my first house, without telling anyone, we ran off to a nearby mountain town to the random and remote Hitching Post. It reminded me of something out of Twin Peaks which was both cool and slightly eerie. I wore a dress that I'm pretty sure was made of felt, carried plastic flowers, and drank screw-top champagne with our strawberry shortcake from Vons grocery store. Since we were living on our eloping-musician budget instead of a post-wedding-at-the-country-club one, we sported unmatching silverware and some furniture off the side of the road, but I found myself mostly okay with that because I had chosen peace instead of pomp and circumstance.

Rock and I lived through a thousand ups and downs that first year of marriage, but we made it through, and here we were 15 years later with two kids that we were told we'd never have. It hasn't been easy, to say the least. But still, all these years later, I melted when I looked at him. I think that's a good sign when you still get butterflies in your stomach when your man walks into the room. Even better when he's singing and washing the dishes.

Washing dishes is foreplay, I swear. I wish more men would figure that out. Yeah, sure you can kill a bison to feed your family for a year – I promise I will give you my mad respect – but if you can occasionally roll up your sleeves while rocking out to some Stevie Wonder tune, oh my gosh, I swear... I'll *swoon*.

So, there I was in the quiet, reflecting on the scripture page in front of me. I read through the list of spiritual qualities and meditated on each one. Without trying, I could see Rock in each characteristic. Which made me feel utterly compelled to wake him up right that moment and tell him in long form. After all, who needs sleep? It's *highly* overrated. At least that's what I told myself night after night of staring at the ceiling. And besides, don't men love when you wake them up for unexpected compliments that could possibly lead to something more? So I stepped softly up the stairs and into our bedroom.

"Rock?" I gently touched his arm that was draped outside the covers and shook it. "*Rockyyyy...*" I said a little louder, my New Jersey accent sneaking out. I jostled him again. He stirred and gazed up at me. What a sight. Me sitting there with a big, cat-eating-a-canary smile, and my eyes filled with expectation. He smiled sleepily at first; then his eyes widened with concern. It hit me that the last time I woke him up like this was to tell him I was pregnant.

I shook my head quickly and motioned my hands in that, *Oh God no... I'm not!* Kind of way. He exhaled and rubbed his eyes... smiling back at me with relief. *Well, there you go, no need for coffee after a jolt like that, right honey?*

"Hey, baby…" He sounded so sexy in the morning. God, I love his voice. A warm rush ran through my body.

He placed his hand over mine. He looked so cozy and delicious, and definitely needed a breath mint.

"Hi, honey." My voice sounded goofy and there was a big, silly grin all over my face. "Look, I know you're sleeping and everything, but I was reading something that made me think of you. I wanna tell you about it right now. You're awake, right?"

Like he had a choice.

I scooched around to get situated on the bed, gave The Man some quick background, and started with the list.

"Love."

"Rock, you're the most loving, warm-hearted, generous person. You massage my back and my feet, and you help people all the time. You forgive so quickly and give me a million chances when I screw up. And you never, ever mention my cellulite." He smiled at me as I talked about his great ways of showing love.

"Joy."

He waited. "Man, you wake up like a happy baby every day. And you go to sleep happy too. It's so nice to be around you. You smile easily and are so much fun to be around." I went on and on waxing poetic about his deep joy.

I moved on…

"Peace." I gazed up into his blue eyes,

"Peace is your middle name. You walk into a room and everything sighs. You're like a walking spa experience."

I went through each of the nine words from the devotional, regaling him about how he embodied every single one of them, while he just laid there with his kind eyes, taking it all in and trying to wake up without breathing in my face.

Rock smiled and pulled me into his warm body. I loved that place. Kissing my forehead he said, "My girl… thank you. Mmm…" He pulled me close as he took it all in and we held each other there for a moment in the quiet. Finally, his voice broke the silence.

"My turn."

Ummm…

I hadn't planned on that. My smile faded a bit.

He straightened out the page and propped himself up higher on the pillow, sporting exaggerated wide eyes to clear them for reading.

"Love."

"Oh yes, you have such love."

I grinned. Thinking he was going to say more, but he moved on.

"Joy."

He scanned my face with a soft smile and curious eyes, "You have…" he paused, "*some* joy."

Rock glanced down at the book I'd handed him but left his gaze there for a moment too long. I squirmed in the silence.

"Peace."

He caught my eyes, and I could tell he was searching for something… *anything* to say. In a small, sad voice, he put his hand over mine and whispered, "Oh baby, you ain't got no peace."

Ugh. My stomach dropped. I was embarrassed to be who I was in the spiritual community, with so many powerful stories of faith under my belt, and still have such an issue with this really important thing. I knew he was right. It just hurt to hear the words out loud.

I forced a tight, awkward smile and snatched the book to close it quickly. We were done. It wasn't his fault, and I didn't want to make him feel badly when I had originally wanted him to feel so loved.

"Rock, would you throw on some coffee?" I tried to make my voice seem as normal as possible. Yes, he made the best cup in the house, but more than that, I needed a moment alone. He got up, with such an easy way about him, kissed the top of my head, and threw on his robe while

I sat on the edge of the bed and pondered.

I wasn't mad at him. And as I thought about it, I realized that I didn't hate hearing him say what he did because I knew he wasn't judging me. But even though it was in the open for us, I just didn't know what to do about it. I felt stuck and judged myself for not figuring it out. Plus, the truth is that not having peace was burdensome and affected everything. The fears that surged as a mom with young kids, the health issues I still had to wrestle, and all those things that other people did with ease felt really hard for me. Things like getting on a plane, or into an elevator, or on the freeway, started becoming so anxiety producing.

This whole not-having-peace thing added to the not-sleeping thing was just not working.

How was I standing on stages talking about this God of Peace that I believed in but was struggling to have for myself?

I wanted it. Oh God, I needed it. And since I had faith, wasn't that just part of the package deal? I mean, I said I believed in God, and He was peaceful. So how come He was and I wasn't?

What was I doing wrong?

I shook my head as I stood up from the bed, trying to loosen the half-processed questions jammed up in there.

Wandering around the room, mindlessly picking up clothes from the bathroom floor, my furrowed brow was quickly forming a dent in my forehead when the words that had been playing over and over in my head came once again.

Be still and know that I am God.

This thought kept coming to me in such a way that it felt like it was haunting me. I had read it in the Bible during my early years, sure, and heard the occasional sermon about it, but I'd never found the recipe for how to do it. Now it was bordering on serious frustration. How many times was I going to get this prescription and not know what to do with it? It seemed like an easy fix to the anxiety I was feeling, but it didn't make any sense. I'd been handed the bottle of healing tonic, but I didn't know how to get the lid off.

What good does that do me, God – to know these words but not understand?

Does 'be still' mean to do nothing? That didn't seem right. How could I do nothing and tend to my responsibilities that required me to do *something*? What was I supposed to do?

Sit in a lotus pose in my living room while my two-year-old figured out how to cook his Buzz Lightyear in the oven and my nine-month-old climbed head-first into the toilet where he liked to practice flushing his Legos? I don't think so.

There had to be something more. Or at the very least something different. But what?

I had no clue, so I did the only thing I had the energy to do: I turned it into a prayer.

God – what does it mean to 'be still?'

It was the only thing I seemed able to pray for during those weeks of giving baths, making meals, piling dishes, and avoiding laundry. In the middle of it all, I still had to finish my talk for Julie's and find an outfit from my 'almost fits' collection that wouldn't land me on the next episode of *What Not to Wear.*

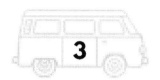

3

Strange Encounters of a Spiritual Kind

"Coincidence is God's way of staying anonymous."

Albert Einstein

The women laughed when they thought I was funny. They dabbed the corners of their eyes when the story was touching, and they closed them when it was time to pray and listen to me sing. It was a special time together and I could hear the murmurs of feeling understood around the room as they sipped their designer coffee. It was always that way when I shared the health problems I overcame and the conception of the children I never should have had.

The stories were true, and even though I knew behind the scenes that other issues were still very unresolved, I was able to earnestly share what I had genuinely overcome. It buoyed my faith to tell them. But I knew the sensation wouldn't last long. I didn't tell them how far I still had to go and how deeply my other fears resided. I didn't tell them that even though I had this vast collection of great stories of faith, I also had this sense that God was either disappointed with me or at least always on the verge of it. I didn't tell them that I was looking for a formula to keep Him happy too – just like they were. Sermon after sermon reminded me that God was pleased when we read the Bible, prayed, went to church, and said "Yes" every time our spouse wanted to have sex. If God was pleased when I did those things, wouldn't that mean He was displeased when I didn't?

But when I shared these miracle stories, something was different... it was like I was in some Eternal Grace bubble where the need for a formula seemed to disappear for just a moment, and love was the prevailing sense in the room. And for a while, it didn't seem like God really needed me to check all the items off my spiritual 'to do' list to make those good things happen. However, I knew that the very human desire to figure things out would hit, and the women would eventually try to find the formula so that they could make God 'happen' too.

They weren't alone. Even though the stories were my own and filled with grace, eventually, I would climb out of my heart and enter my over-analytical head and try to find a formula too.

This thought consumed me for a moment, but then, my mind drifted away to my favorite distraction – food – and I wondered if, before the baby woke up, there would be a croissant left with my name on it and a cup of coffee with heavy cream just waiting to be mine.

Too late.

The cries came like clockwork. I guess I should have been grateful that my little one slept during the presentation. Even though I was tempted to run to grab the pastry, I opted for being the good mom and found a corner of the room unoccupied and began to unstrap Seth from his baby rocker. My sweet boy was staring up into my tired mommy eyes.

"Well, at least one of us is going to get to eat." I smiled at my little Seth, "I should thank you. You probably just saved me from a scrillion calories... *yes, you did!*" I whispered in my best baby voice as I got him latched on. I was still cooing at my second born when I felt someone standing beside the ottoman I was sitting on.

She was a study in contrast. The other women were dressed in the colors of a Spring bouquet; she was dressed in black. They had applied tasteful makeup onto the canvas of their weekly European facials; her face was naked – which made her deep blue eyes pop with even more intensity against her pale skin. She looked like she was having a real estate issue: Her tall, thin frame and translucent skin would have fit better on the edge of some craggy cliff in Scotland. Cue the Enya music and fog machine and the picture would be complete. She definitely stood out in this gathering of sorority sisters.

But she wasn't in Scotland. She was standing here.

With me.

In Southern California.

Staring.

God, she's so close. How can someone so skinny take up so much space?

I leaned to the side a little, trying to give myself some emotional elbow room. I waited. Then, I waited some more, smiling that weak, awkward way you do when you're not sure why someone who approached you isn't talking. A few more uncomfortable seconds passed before she finally broke the silence.

"I really liked your talk."

"Thank you," I said and nodded with a little too much bounce. I felt like one of those bobble-head dolls, overcompensating for her lack of social pulse. There was another long pause.

"I see you're nursing your son." I nodded again, more slowly this time. There was an even longer pause. Apparently she was a woman of few words. I wondered if she might be related to my husband.

"I was a German missionary for three years."

I blinked.

It was official. She lost me.

I couldn't tell if it was my hormonal, sleep-deprived brain or if it was her, but I couldn't find the bridge for this conversation. She liked my talk. I was nursing my son. She was a German missionary. Or was that a missionary in Germany? Either way, I stared at my feet and then hers. We both desperately needed a pedicure.

"You know," she said in a warm, clear way, as if I had asked her a question, "the German word for nursing is 'stillen'." She paused again.

"That's where we get our English phrase 'to be still'." The sentence went by so quickly as I was busy mentally criticizing her unpolished toes again when I realized what the heck she was saying, *Mmmm... wait... what...?* My mind clicked from autopilot into high gear.

"I'm sorry, what did you say?" She cleared her throat and paused for what seemed like hours. She was on a completely different plane in the time/space continuum.

"In Germany, where I was a missionary, I took care of babies at an orphanage. There were women who came in and nursed the babies. I learned that the German word for nursing is 'stillen'."

She gave a silent beat with her head.

"They taught me that in English it means to 'be still'."

I searched deeply into her warm, blue eyes. How could she know... this prayer I'd been praying for almost a month? I'd never seen this woman in my life, but she was a messenger to me. Albeit a strange one, but a messenger nonetheless. I turned my gaze down toward my son, trying to process what I had just heard. I wanted to ask her to tell me what she knew, but I couldn't even think of a question to ask.

Which was probably best, because by the time I looked back up, she was walking out Julie's front door.

I closed the door as quietly as I could, backing out of the boys' bedroom of our cozy townhome. I had gotten everything wrapped up at Julie's, and the kids were napping.

Finally.

I was trying so hard to not even jangle the knob the tiniest little bit, but something moved and Caleb stirred.

"Shhhhhhhhh..." I scolded myself. The Pink Panther theme music started playing in my head and I'm sure I looked like a crazy person crouching and sneaking around like a thief in my own home. As I let go of the doorknob, so focused on the boys' room in front of me, I had no idea that when I turned around, my husband would be standing there, silent and still as a statue and scaring the crap out of me.

"Good Lord, Rock!" I whisper-yelled at him and slapped him on the chest, "I almost peed in my pants right here!"

He just stood there, smiling like some crazed stalker in a horror movie.

"Whaaa?" he laughed and held out his hands innocently.

Stinker. No fair scaring the poop out of someone who is on her last nerve.

"SHHHHH..." I pushed him back down toward the stairs. "Don't you wake them up!" My eyes spoke clearly that he'd be in some serious trouble if he did. He turned around on the landing and walked down the steps toward the living room with me close behind. I could see his shoulders moving up and down with laughter. So, I playfully hit him again and pushed him toward the kitchen.

"Okay." I began whispering like we were in the middle of a bank heist, "I'm going to 17th Street to the mailbox, the credit union, and the dry cleaners, Trader Joe's, the other bank to pay the car payment, and the tailors. Did I say that already? Anyway, you? You stay *here.*"

Rocky nodded, "I'll do the dishes."

My eyes bugged open. "Have you lost your mind? You wake up those kids and I'm going to send you to the moon. They'll be cranky all afternoon and that means *I'll* be cranky all afternoon."

He winked. "I'm just kidding. I'll do something quiet, like pull the laundry off the ceiling and fold it. You go, do your errands. And go relax. Get a pedicure." He was so easy, and yet he made me so crazy.

I peeked up at the clock and did some nursing math. I had two hours left before the next feeding. A pedicure was only in my dreams, but I appreciated the thought. I kissed him quickly on the lips.

"You're my man. Thank you."

He kissed me back longer and got all dreamy-eyed. "I want you." He pulled my body close.

I met his loving gaze, narrowed my eyes and said dryly, "Take a number."

———————————

I kept reminding myself to breathe as I headed onto Irvine Avenue toward 17th Street. That zingy sensation from not enough sleep was a constant companion, and the wife-guilt that came from knowing the basics hadn't been taken care of, like alone time with my husband, washed over me. *He wants me, and I want a nap. Sigh.*

"In with the good air…" I tried to breathe my way through, but the anxiety escalated, just like it always did. *Distract yourself, Stacey. Take your mind off yourself.*

A plane was taking off from John Wayne Airport into yet another perfect California sky. Lots of blue, a few high clouds, and up ahead on the left horizon, the wildlife preserve. Sanctioned acres of beauty and quiet in the midst of all the busy-ness and multi-million-dollar homes.

I exhaled just a little. I loved it here, and yet, a part of me was always planning my escape back to the East Coast.

The best parts of Southern California are the beaches and the mild weather all year long. The people are inspiring and affable, whether they're big business moguls, well-known celebrities, or relaxed surfer types. We had great friends, a good business, and a long string of possibilities forever waiting in the wings – constantly one connection away from someone who could take our career to the next level if that's what we wanted. I loved all that. But it was busy in unexpected ways, especially in Orange County, known by the TV viewing public as "The OC."

Orange County is unique. We're the mostly conservative suburb of edgy LA, but it's a completely different vibe than New York. When you land in NYC, you expect there to be a fast pulse, city streets, and black suits. You land in a city and you expect city pace. It matches. But when you land in Orange County, you're bathed in sunshine and surrounded by guys in Tommy Bahama shirts and Havaiana flip flops, carrying a green drink.

But don't be deceived: You expect laid back and get hyper-drive instead. High-speed freeways, high-speed relation-ships, and high-speed business dealings. The jolt is shocking because it's unexpected. Yup. We may look like we're grooving at a vacation pace, but we're not. The OC is a high-performance area. People with a strong sense of innovation, competition, and excellence live and thrive here. There's a lot of new money, and people move at the speed that money demands.

Rock and I had talked about moving back east near New Jersey where I am from. I'd regaled him with countless stories about 'real' food and how people back there are more straightforward than in SoCal. "You mean they stab you in the middle of the forehead instead of the back like here?" he'd say. He thinks he's so funny.

I like when I'm back east... able to have a bump on my nose or curvy hips and have people know I'm Italian instead of looking at me like I don't know a plastic surgeon. The Northeast is a place where you can wear a sleeveless shirt without someone handing you the name of their personal trainer. I missed that.

Sigh.

But the mosquitoes and the humid summers which segue far too quickly into the depressing winters that make you want to end your life? Not so much.

The people, the food, the Fall, and that ineffable quality that's distinctly its own, are what I missed. And in the back of my mind, I wondered if I were there, would life slow down a little so I could catch up? But my easy-going husband was firmly planted in California, and he did not want to move. He was adamant.

"God," I found myself in conversation as I drove. "Come on, You're big enough to change Rock's mind... Can't You just make him want to move?" I started to negotiate out loud.

"If You move me there, then I could have peace." It was a proud moment for me, feeling a little like I had trumped God with my logic. He wanted me to be still, and I had the answer: Moving back 'home.'

I checked out my smug pride in the rearview mirror. Really, I mean, how could He argue with me wanting peace? I nodded to myself and drove through the S-curves by the Back Bay feeling pretty self-satisfied when these voiceless words moved through me:

If you can have peace here, I can move you anywhere.

I slowed at the green light, distracted by all the air leaving my body. That smug feeling was gone. I felt deflated as the air of pride went right out of me, and a humble, peaceful feeling replaced it.

Wait a minute. Did that come from me or was that God?

The car behind me honked and I stumbled to press my gas pedal as the impatient driver swerved around me.

I wasn't sure, but either way, I felt the truth of that conviction in my chest as I pulled into the right turn lane.

Peace.

I felt brave in asking for it, but the thought of actually having it was completely foreign. It had been a perfect stranger to me for such a long time and for so many perfectly understandable and horrifying reasons.

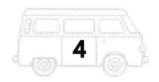

4

The Incident, Jesus, and the Woman with the Big Hair

"Jesus does not give recipes that show the way to God..."

Karl Barth

I remember kneeling in the church when I was about seven years old. The smell of incense enchanted me and suffocated me all at the same time. I was trying so hard to be like the grown-ups who didn't lean their backside lazily on the bench behind them as we kids were prone to. They knelt as a sign of sacrificial devotion to Christ on the cross, so I knelt ramrod straight right along with them.

I wanted to be such a good girl.

The priest was leading the prayers of intentions for the church, the nation, and the sick of our congregation. After each prayer he prayed, we all responded with, "Lord, hear our prayer."

"Now, please take a moment for your intentions." He invited the parish into the silence.

I bowed my head and squinted my eyes, praying a mix of Ben Franklin's words and some of my own:

Lord, make me healthy, wealthy and wise. And if something bad is going to happen to anyone in my family, let it happen to me.

His voice echoed from the altar: "We offer this intention in the name of the Lord."

And I heard my voice declare with all the others, "Lord, hear our prayer."

I was 12 in 1981, the summer we moved – from my huge pink bedroom with a pink princess phone in the estates nestled in the mountains of New Jersey, overlooking the yard and the deer that came each morning – to the ugly rented house in a more affordable suburb that attracted commuters to Manhattan, with my dingy white room that overlooked our garage.

I had been through a couple of very hard years – the hand injury that led to stitches, the slipped collar bone that led to the sling, and then, when I was nine, the accident at my beloved grandmother's house. I ran into her kitchen with stocking feet and lost my balance, which left me sliding into her feet as if she were third base, just as she was turning around with a huge pot of boiling water from the stove. The fiery water landed all over me, which landed me in the burn unit and hospital for over a month with first, second, and third-degree burns all over my head and shoulders.

And now, instead of being in the tranquility of the mountains, we were here where everything was unfamiliar. It felt like a different kind of tragedy to be the new middle school transfer. Clanging lockers slamming and kids screaming back and forth jangled my nerves only slightly less than the cliques of straight-hipped, straight-haired girls with snobby attitudes who bullied me. Their groups didn't include girls like me who had wavy hair, full bras, and curvy hips. Being the new kid was hard. Even after being here for six weeks, I hadn't found my way. The final bell rang, and I headed to my locker.

Made it through another day. Time to get the hell outta here.

Eighth graders can be so cruel sometimes.

At least I had Mandy.

Mandy and I became best friends after our move into her neighborhood that summer. She was an only child with a lot of time to hang out and talk about all the taboo subjects that I couldn't share with my little sisters. We were often mistaken for 16-year-olds and got attention from the older boys – which we liked. When we didn't feel like taking the bus, we'd walk that mile and a half, singing songs from Rush, Meatloaf, and Karen Carpenter as we talked about the cute boys who were interested in the popular girls. Which we were not. Mandy was fun, and she was introducing me to her friends like Billy.

I leaned my head against my locker, replaying that first day I met him…

"Hey Billy!" Mandy waved. It eased my mind that she knew him. The Northeast is famous for the kind of overcast days that could easily be the setting for an Edgar Allen Poe story – slightly depressing with a sense of grey dread in the air. The park was surrounded by woods and trails that were fine on a sunny Saturday, but on days like today, I'd feel vulnerable if I weren't with my friend.

Billy stood there, leaning casually, in his blue jeans and a black, long-sleeved shirt with a heavy metal band. He gave a short wave and an easy smile.

"What's up, girls?" His voice had a gritty texture. My stomach fluttered.

Ooh, he's cute. His rugged strong looks grabbed me. I guessed he was a high school senior. Mandy turned to me with a quick whisper, "My cousin's friend used to date him. I forgot he works here after school."

"Mmm…" I raised my eyebrows and smiled.

Mandy jumped right in, all chatty, and flirty. When Billy spoke, I felt this excitement just being around him. He joked with us as if we were peers. I liked that, but I felt overwhelmed by his presence. The way he locked his eyes with mine felt like he was testing me.

We were just about to leave when Billy stopped us. "Wait, girls. I have something for you." He reached down into a bag on the ground nearby and stood up with his fist clasped shut.

"Open your hands," he said. Billy dropped two little white circles into Mandy's hand. I squinted to see what he had placed in hers while I slowly opened my fingers. His hand brushed mine and electricity rushed through my body.

"They'll make you feel really good." He said with a wink as he put the pills into my palm.

But words from another place issued a warning throughout my body.

This will be the end of you.

My shoulders shuddered as I caught Billy's eye.

"Ummm...no thanks." I tried to hand them back to Billy, but Mandy grabbed them and said, "I'll take them!" It was too late to stop her, so I grabbed her arm instead. "C'mon, Mand, we gotta get home." I pulled again at her ski jacket. "Billy, uh... it was... nice meeting you," I said as I backed up. I glanced up just in time to see Billy's intense eyes staring back. The way he looked at me made me feel more womanly than I had ever felt before.

"Nice to meet you, too, Stacey. I'll see you again." He sounded confident, and something inside me hoped he was right.

The heavy clanking of lockers echoed in the hall, interrupting my daydream. I lifted the handle of my locker only to find it was already released. *That's weird.* I knew I locked it. I pulled it open and saw a note sitting on my books. *Who knows my combination?* Maybe it was one of those obnoxious girls who cornered me in the bathroom last week. I turned to see if anyone was watching me, but the halls were filled with the chaos of junior-highers whose bell had just rung for dismissal. No one was looking at me in an obvious way. I leaned my upper body into the metal cave for some privacy.

The paper was folded in half and read, "Meet me after school with this." Inside was a small, packaged square. Confused, I turned it over and back again. My stomach dropped. It was a condom.

Mandy's cousin had shown us one of these a few weeks before, so I knew what it was. Older cousins got to be big shots when they shared things that shocked their younger cousins and their friends. I shivered at the thought of someone watching me and spent the next week avoiding being alone.

My favorite diversion was walking through the park and stopping for short conversations with Billy. I looked forward to those the most.

Today, Mandy was 10 paces ahead of me and called from over her shoulder, "Sta! I gotta get home or my mom's gonna kill me!" Scrambling to keep up with her, I heard the sound of footsteps in the gravel behind me. It was Robbie, Billy's best friend, tall and athletic with a shock of white blond hair – one of the heartthrobs of the football team.

He came alongside me while Mandy moved further ahead.

Robbie leaned in close, "Did you get my note?"

My heart pounded so hard I almost couldn't hear him.

"That was... *you*?" I choked out a whisper.

He nodded with a glint in his eye, "Yeah, but it's not from me. It's from someone who wants to get to know you... *better.*"

That someone was obvious, and his idea of better made my whole body tremble. All that warmth and excitement I felt for Billy turned to an icy chill as I started putting the pieces together. Robbie turned and jogged away.

And without realizing it, I began to run.

Brrrrrng. Brrrrrng. I was in my room peeling off my Halloween cat costume from my pink, frost-bitten skin when the phone began ringing on the kitchen wall. My father wanted to trick-or-treat longer than the rest of us kids, but my mother pulled him back into reality, and we headed back home when all three sisters had blue lips and chattering teeth.

I heard my mother say to whoever was on the other end, "She's right here. Hold on. *Staceeeeey!*"

My room was removed from the rest of our little house. The only grace in being nearly a teenager with a diary and a nosy middle sister. Looking at the back window toward the farm field was one of my favorite things to do. It was quiet, and I could always see the moon. Tonight it was mostly hidden, the sky a blanket of darkness.

I padded down the hall toward the phone. My mother was standing there, with her Natalie Wood beauty with dark hair, and dark eyes – in full contrast to my blonde hair and blue eyes – had a quizzical look on her face, covering the mouthpiece with her hand and leaning toward me in a hushed whisper. "It sounds like it's coming from a pay phone?" I shrugged my shoulders. I was genuinely confused, not knowing who it was either.

"*Hello?*" I said with a curious tone. Click. The line went dead. I waited a second and hung up. It rang again.

"*Who is this?*" I asked. All I heard was the rhythmic, heavy breathing on the other end and my heart pounding inside my chest. "*Hello?*" Click. My stomach dropped. After two more times the phone stopped ringing.

"Who was that, Sta?" My mom asked, concerned.

"I don't know. Halloween pranks, I guess." I set the phone slowly into its cradle with a sick feeling settling in and rested a protective hand over my stomach. "You need some real food after all that candy." My mother said. I took some time in the kitchen to eat the turkey sandwich she put in front of me as I told her a little about how the neighbors "ooh-ed" and "ahh-ed" at our costumes. She smiled and it took her mind off the prank calls. I walked back to my bedroom thinking that maybe I should've told her... but when I pushed open the door, a cold rush of air hit me, distracting me from that thought.

I didn't leave that window open. *Errgggh...Little sisters. How many times do I have to tell them to stay out of my room?*

Tightening my robe around me with one arm, I headed toward the window. A rustling in the field nearby distracted me. It was hard to see anything. As I leaned close to the window for a better look, a strong hand grabbed me around my waist and another covered my mouth.

"Shhh... it's me," the raspy whisper pierced me. I knew that voice. My chest tightened.

His breath was in my ear and his hand still tight over my mouth. I moved my head toward the sound of my parents in the living room.

"You say anything..." The threat was implied.

I nodded, feeling my rapid, hot breath under his hand. He turned me around, pulling my ponytail back and forced a hard kiss on my lips where his hand had been – his unshaven face burning my skin. In two quick steps, the bed was underneath me. My mind focused on the sounds in the next room where the distinct theme to the evening news played in the background. My parents watched the news every night before they went to bed.

That's how I knew it was 11:00 when Billy raped me.

The flashing red lights brought me back to the construction on 17th Street where I was sitting in my car. I opened my window in time to hear the church bells from St. Andrews waft on the salty SoCal coastal breeze. The familiar ringing of church bells brought me comfort. And confusion.

I remember hearing the church bells during the times that Billy raped me behind the rectory – something he continued doing for months — telling me in his demented voice that he wanted to give me a baby for my 13th birthday — before he eventually got bored with torturing me and disappeared back into the shadows of his dark world. With a smile, he'd threaten to hurt my younger sisters if I uttered even a word. There was no way I was going to let that happen.

I had already invested my life in keeping them safe.

And keeping secrets.

Because I had to do that at home, too.

Life behind the closed doors of our family was much different than what outsiders saw.

Though my dad was an incredibly bright, funny, and hard-working man who loved us all deeply, he had his own childhood demons that haunted him. The Type 1 diabetes seemed to be an access point for the rage that would overcome him when his blood sugars would sink or soar. I, as the oldest child, was on the lookout for those days when the stress of the office, or my parents' relationship – or the overindulgence in food – would send him over the edge. I could feel the rumblings of the volcano before he even walked in the house. That clenching in my stomach. The feeling that my house was the jungle surrounding the simmering volcano. Every survival instinct kicked in while I quietly ran from room to room gathering my sisters to get them to safety. Not every day was like that, but there were enough to make you unsure which kind of day it would be.

One time, after watching a school assembly where the presenters were trying to encourage the audience of kids, like me, to reach out and ask for help. I risked reaching out to my very favorite teacher in 4th grade with wavy hair like mine and caring blue eyes. I came home and learned to never do that again when my mother dragged hard on her cigarette between her tight, angry lips, "What happens under this roof stays under this roof, and if you have a problem, you tell it to your pillow."

I understood what my family expected of me: No matter what happened to me, keep the silence.

And now, there was Billy…

I couldn't talk about it at home, or school, or even church. My parents were always involved with the parish – and the priests who sat and heard my confessions on Saturdays had been served my mother's finest Italian fare at our house on Friday nights. I couldn't risk telling them or them telling my parents. Plus, God knew – and if He didn't see fit to do anything to stop all this from happening, what was anyone else going to do?

So, I covered the dark circles from the sleeplessness and wore baggy clothes to cover the weight loss. I had left my body – and my heart – in those months when the hopelessness had set in, never shedding another tear. I entered the world of my head. My time was spent trying to figure out how to keep my double life going so that I could stay alive in this unsafe world.

Because as long as I was alive, then I could keep my sisters safe from the bad things that were happening to me.

I was now 13 years-old, and it was exhausting just to try to make it through each day. I needed a refuge.

_____

That's when I found Jesus.

After months of torture, Billy released me, as if he were the cat leaving a half-dead mouse on the doorstep as he went on to his next victim. I was lost inside of myself, wandering through a life that I no longer fit into or could make any sense of.

A life I couldn't tell anyone about and didn't know how to process on my own.

I needed something. I stopped eating as a way to control life, became promiscuous to feel a sense of power in my otherwise powerless world, and started sneaking into my parents' liquor cabinet to numb the pain that had started to plague me. All of these things were my drugs of choice but I needed something more… something that wouldn't wear off.

I had never really stopped believing in Jesus, actually. I just figured he didn't care about me. I mean, how could he care for someone who was ruined the way that I was? I must have been some bad girl, deserving this punishment for some reason.

Or maybe he was answering my prayer. That one from when I was little, when I prayed that if any bad things were going to happen, they would happen to me. Maybe then my sisters would be spared those bad things, and possibly even worse...

There was some odd comfort in that for me.

But why would God answer that prayer and not my prayers on those many nights I had asked Him to keep me safe?

I didn't understand God, but still my combination of genuine spiritual connection and desperate need overrode my logic about a God who wouldn't help me or want me. There was still some deeper hope in me.

I was curious about what was happening in our church – the whispers about a new little group that was forming in our Catholic community. One night after mid-week catechism, I peeked into the basement downstairs. While the upstairs was filled with organ music, Latin masses, and wooden pews surrounded by stained glass windows, the plain white-walled basement was filled with folding chairs and people singing and clapping, raising their hands and closing their eyes. They seemed happy and alive, something I didn't feel inside of me at all.

Each week, I'd listen in from the fringe of the cold, metal chairs by the basement door. I heard about a Jesus you could trust. A Jesus who would heal. A Jesus who would forgive... and make you clean again.

Oh, to be clean again...

The group leader said that all we had to do was say, "Yes! To Jeee-sus!"

After weeks of feeling that stirring of new wonder in my heart, I did say "yes" to this version of Jesus that made me feel befriended and safe. This happier version of Jesus. Happier than the one on the cross. Friendlier than the one on the Mass cards. More present than the one with eerily vacant eyes on the painted icons.

The closeness of God comforted me. It was beautiful, and some of my heart healed. In some ways instantly, and in other ways, over time. I forgave Billy for what he had done, I forgave my parents for not knowing. And I forgave myself for still not telling them and for still being afraid. I had a new start.

Something really beautiful was happening with this Jesus.

I lay in bed night after night, savoring that clean feeling and clinging to that new start. I was given a youth Bible and it became my best friend. It was covered with pink, frosty, Covergirl lipstick because I kissed it with gratitude and held it close each night as if absorbing its comfort just by holding it against my chest, the way I would have held a teddy bear if I had been able to remain a child. I was finally able to sleep again.

I wrote my first songs about this new love. The music of faith entered my soul and was singing through me. It lifted me to put this love into words. Even my parents noticed something different, and the air was different in our home.

It went on like this for months without telling anyone about my "Yes." It was my private treasure as I experienced this deep closeness with God. Feeling clean. Feeling hope. Feeling safe on the inside. Instead of hiding under the covers like when I was a little kid afraid of the dark, now I was covered in this soft, protective warmth inside of me and

I felt braver to deal with the darkness that seemed more outside than within me.

When I finally told someone, news got to Carol, the leader of the basement meetings, and she wanted to meet with me right away. Her personal mission was to help me live in this new world with Jesus.

"Now, Stacey, you just have to pray this way." Her bleach-blonde hair with its high tease distracted me, and I found myself staring, imagining all the things that could get lost or the small creatures that could find a home inside of the hair-sprayed nest sitting on top of her head. But she kept bringing me back to reality with my assignments as she slapped her hand on the table for effect:

Read your Bible!

Pray these prayers!

Hand out tracts!

Talk this way!

Think this way!

Dress this way!

Believe this way!

There was so much more. The list of how to live went on and on, along with all the things that I needed to do so I wouldn't get dirty again. It was overwhelming, but I listened carefully because her version of God seemed just as easily angered as my version did, and I didn't want to be punished any more – which she told me God would do – only because He loved me so much.

Which was confusing and it wasn't. Because that's what life was like at home – a place where there was love and threatening punishment – but it was all called 'love', and it left me never really feeling safe.

Maybe this was just God. Maybe this was just life...

Then, she'd wink at me and smile before bowing her head in prayer.

And those old feelings – the ones I had at home with my parents and behind the rectory with Billy – started in my stomach again.

Sitting with Carol was taking the life out of my faith. There were so many rules about how to be a good girl when I thought I could just be a clean girl.

A free girl after being in such a prison.

But now, there were all these rules, and I found myself leaving my heart and climbing up into the jail cell of my head again. Thinking and re-thinking the right and wrong ways to live so that I didn't make any new mistakes to piss off God.

It seemed like this good God was only good as long as I was.

And this 'beautiful Jesus' thing that made me feel so special and clean became like the old pieces of silver flatware that your great-grandmother passes down: You want to love them, but you don't feel like you can get too close since they seem to tarnish the moment you touch them. You groan to think of the coming holiday because even though that silver is so pretty and so special, it requires so much effort to keep it clean.

That's how I began to feel about Jesus. Like maybe he'd be better off in some felted drawer than in my hands or in my heart.

This 'beautiful Jesus' thing had just become a whole lot of work.

The grocery bag straps were balanced in my left hand, the dry-cleaning in my right, and the mail was tucked under my armpit. Trying to unlock the deadbolt had quickly turned into an extreme sport.

I slowly opened the door to find Rock sitting there, in the middle of the newly-cleaned living room, with two little boys. "Momma's home!" Rock whispered. Caleb clapped and giggled, and Seth smiled so big that the binkie fell out of his mouth.

Such love in this house.

I could see the love here, and I was touched by the idea of it on some level beneath the fatigue. But I was plagued by that gnawing feeling that I'd had since I was a child, the one I didn't dare share with anyone:

That if I opened my heart to trust and relax in the love that was there, it would be gone. The other shoe would drop. Something bad would happen.

It kept me in this horrible cycle: If I got too close to love, I would lose it; but if I protected my heart from losing it, I would never have it.

Even when I could recognize it as a horrible, defeating pattern, I still didn't know how to change it.

Who would I talk to about it?

The pastors who hired me to care for the women in their church?

The women who came to listen to me and were trusting that I knew more about God than they did?

The friends who were counting on me to be the strong one like I always had been?

The family members who were judging me and wanting me to fail?

Keeping the secret is what kept me awake in bed so many nights – just like when I was a child and the worries and fears would crash like cymbals in my head, leaving me overwhelmed with the noise of life but not the music of it.

Am I ever going to be able to know real love and feel it?

Was I ever going to stop feeling like my family was visiting me in prison, and all I could do was look at them as I put my hand up to the glass in between us?

I wished I could tell Rock about these thoughts that were coming stronger than ever since the kids had been born – and worsening as the fatigue increased – but it wouldn't make sense. Sometimes I was completely fine, especially when I was doing something like helping a friend or counseling a woman or speaking at an event. It was the alone times… the rare ones during the day or the frequent ones through the long, overwhelming sleepless nights, when my mind would spin and not stop.

It wasn't just the questions that kept me spinning; it was the shame. This feeling that I should know better and that I was bad for not knowing. That I should have figured life and God out by now and that somehow everyone was going to be exasperated with me and then, leave me alone and unloved – confirming my worst fears: that I wasn't worth loving. So, I hid from people while being with them. You'd think then, that the most honest place you could go to be your naked self, was with God, but I found myself couching my questions even with Him.

Especially with Him.

Other people could reward me for what they didn't know about me, but God? He could punish me.

That warm bliss from Julie's house a few hours before had already faded away. Back again were the private checklists in my head. Of 'good' and 'bad,' 'right' and 'wrong' – wondering where I stood with God.

Rock took the bags from me, and I hugged the little people as they squeezed me tight around my knees. They were amazing souls. I saw such light and love in them, and I felt a temporary flash of connection. But then the familiar ache set in. I wanted to be close, but something… something I could not name… was keeping me from the closeness I so desperately desired.

I stared into my youngest son's eyes and knew.

Something has to change.

It just *has* to.

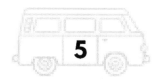

5

Who Are You and Where Are You Taking Me?

"Without change, something sleeps inside us, and seldom awakens.
The sleeper must awaken."
Frank Herbert

Here I was, finally ready to plant my feet more firmly in California, when with one turn of his heel, Rock had set us on a new course.

It all happened when The Man and I went out for a rare afternoon date alone. We headed to lunch at the ultra-sophisticated South Coast Plaza where you could dress in gold lame or chic hand-me-down jeans from the thrift store and both would be perfectly acceptable. I was showered and wearing my good flip flops. This would have to do.

"Honey, can we go to Nordy's and get my makeup done?" I put on my snooty voice.

"Of course, dahling," he played right along, sounding more like Thurston Howell III from Gilligan's Island than a rich Orange County socialite. He put the credit card down to pay the check for our lunch.

We strolled, arm-in-arm, down the marble walkways to Nordstrom's. No sticky jelly fingers to hold on to. No sagging diapers begging to be changed. No crying children to comfort.

Kind of like heaven.

This was such a nutty season in our lives. We didn't ask questions like, "Hi! How are you?" Nope. After the endless sleeplessness and bumping into hallways at all hours of the night with one kid or the other in our arms, it was more like:

"Hi! *Who* are you?"

It was nice to be doing something frivolous.

Together.

We needed it.

The gal at the MAC counter led me to the high director's chair, and when she leaned close to study my face, I could smell hints of orange blossom, mint gum, and Marlboro Lights. She looked sexy, decked out in her all-black clothing and red-carpet make-up — definitely ready for her close-up, Mr. DeMille, while I was decidedly not.

"So, what feature would you like to focus on today?"

One? You may not see me again 'til my kids graduate college. This is monumental that I'm even sitting here right now. Can't we do them all?

I didn't feel brave enough to ask, so I just avoided answering and went off on my own tangent.

"Look, I'm a mom of two little boys. I can't remember the last time I looked…"

I couldn't find the word. *Normal? Put together? Stylish?*

I settled for 'good.'

"I can't remember the last time I looked… *good.*" I waved my hand down my body like I was Vanna White, showing off a car accident. The makeup artist nodded sadly in agreement and started working her MAC magic on me. I saw her nametag. It read *Andrahnea.*

Seriously? Does anyone in Southern California have a normal name? She leaned in close with the mascara wand.

"Open halfway," she said. I did, and then I instinctively opened my mouth, which I vaguely remember making fun of my grandmother for doing the same thing when I watched her apply her eye makeup when I was a kid.

Good Lord, I'm getting old.

Out of the corner of my eye, I could see The Man peering into the glass counter, checking out some cologne. When he was done, he stood up tall, surveying all the baubles, bangles, and boob jobs and did a 360 on his heel. Then, letting out a long exhale I heard him say, "I'm ready, Sta."

"Ready for what, babe?" I said in that funny half-opened eye, half-opened mouth kind of way. She wasn't working on my lips, but I forgot I could speak normally.

"I'm just ready… ready to leave."

"Hon, she's only got one eye done. Can she at least finish the other one so I don't look like a Picaso?"

He stared through me, taking a second to wake up and connect with what I was saying.

"Oh no… no, sorry… you're fine. I mean I'm ready to leave California."

I blinked right onto the mascara wand, which turned me into Liza Minnelli and gave me a rotten sting in my eye that instantly teared up. Andrahnea handed me a tissue and a distinct sigh, "Oh, that's okay." She assured me with a courtesy pat on the shoulder, but I heard her clear exasperation as she sucked in the air through her teeth – a skill I'm sure she perfected on her smoke breaks. I didn't care.

"Really, Rock? You're serious?" I struggled to get out of the director's chair — I wanted to get a closer look at him.

"Yeah." He exhaled again, "It's time."

Wow. I did not see that one coming. This was great. Really great!

Now all we needed was a place to go.

And we barely blinked before an opportunity appeared.

———————————

"What are you doing?" Rocky stared at me while I was staring at myself in the mirror at Nordstrom Rack, the discounted version of the fancy store we had been at a few months before when he had his 'aha!' moment. I was turning side-to-side admiring the dramatic grey-and-black leopard print Audrey Hepburn-style winter hat I had just tried on…

In the middle of a classic sunny 70-degree California October day.

His question was reasonable.

To which I had a completely unreasonable answer: "It's my 'East Coast in January' hat!" I said. Those words just fell right out of my mouth. It was the first time I had thought of it, but that was the answer that sounded right to me for some reason.

"What? Wait... what are you talking about, Stace? Do you know something I don't know..."

"No." I shook my head. "It just hit me in this strong *feeling* kind of way that we're going to be on the East Coast in January!"

Rock was used to me having some inspired moments like this. We couldn't explain it, and while he respected me in these times, I respected his right to be skeptical.

Which he was at that moment, staring at me with his furrowed brow.

"Have you prayed about it?"

I shook my head, still thinking I looked adorable in my hat.

"You pray about it," he said, "And I'll think about it."

It was two days later when he called to me from the living room,

"Hey Stasha, who's this Kathryn person?"

He was at my computer trying to set up my email program while I was juggling the kids to get them fed before we went for the Halloween event at our church that night. I was trying to feed Caleb the pasta in a highchair and Seth some yogurt and peach sauce balanced on my lap. It was like a circus act. Caleb realized, by mistake, that if he squeezed the tube-like pasta hard enough, it would shoot out of his fist in different directions all over the room. He began doing it with every piece of pasta he could get within the grasp of his slippery little hands, which threw the brothers into absolute giggles.

I had to put the kibosh on the self-feeding two-year-old and take over so that he could actually get some food *inside* of his body. It was a mess, but they were so happy. They clapped with every bite.

God, I hope they're this much fun to be with when they're teenagers.

"Kathryn? Hmmm… give me something more." My brain was mushy.

"From New York?" He was reading.

"Oh! Kathryn?" It had taken a minute to hit my brain, "Yeah. She's that Methodist minister who I met a few years ago." I wiped some pasta off of the blinds on the back window.

"She was the one who liked my music and said that she would look for opportunities for us to work together in the future. We've been in touch on and off throughout the years, but we haven't talked since before Seth was born."

"Ummm… well, she's invited us to come do music at this new church in upstate New York."

I walked into the room where he was sitting and just watched him.

He paused and squinted and then moved closer to the computer screen to be sure…

"… in January."

Holy moley.

"Sta," he was incredulous, "she says that she wants us to come out and do our music and speaking events for the entire month of January." He paused, accentuating each word as he absorbed the shock of it all. "And if we like it, it

70

would turn into a two-year assignment. Says the little church is in need of 'new life' and wants to bring us out from California to help her with that."

Caleb and Seth were still clapping, and I would have too, but I was busy making my list of things to pack.

- Winter boots.
- Gloves.
- Snow pants for the boys...

I couldn't stop smiling as I kept writing. Not only because we were finally going back to my old stomping grounds, but because I had bought my 'East Coast in January' hat for just this occasion.

"I can't believe you're leaving." Julie was standing in my kitchen, wrapping up wine glasses and shaking her head. She put the glass down in the carton and sighed, then gazed sadly into my eyes, "Oh Stacey! I'm not ready for you to go!"

I was going to say something but lost my train of thought when Julie's mom walked in with an entire box already packed. She grabbed another empty one.

"Agnes, do I have to wait until I'm 80 to have your kind of energy?? What's your secret?" She just waved her hand at me and winked in that 'I'll never tell' sort of way.

"Now, Stacey, Julie didn't tell me how this all happened. One minute you're staying forever and the next minute you're leaving?"

I smiled. I couldn't blame her. We all had whiplash from this turn of events.

Julie patiently stood there while I filled her mom in on both of the Nordstrom stories.

"So, that's how it happened, Agnes. It felt sort of… well, *miraculous*. We took a trip out with the family to check out the church – did music for a few weeks in January, and we decided to go for it! It was a little weird, trust me, living in the boondocks with some interesting folks. But we just can't explain how it all fell together so effortlessly. Seems like a God thing."

She locked eyes with me, "We're going to miss you, Stacey. My Julie here is really going to miss you." She rubbed the middle of her daughter's back to comfort her.

I felt the rush of tears to my eyes as I reached out to hug Julie, who was tearing up too.

"It's okay, Julie-babooli," I whispered in my dear friend's ear, "We'll be back before you know it." I pulled back and looked at Julie, "Between your inherited agelessness," I winked at Agnes, "and the fact that my kids will still officially be preschoolers by the time we return, not much will change. Seriously, Jules." I assured her with my eyes meeting hers, "How much could change in just two years? It will be just like we never left."

"Oh, Stacey…" she sighed.

I was sighing, too. Even though I wanted this more than anything, the reality hit me: I was going to be the new kid on the block again. That junior high feeling came over me for just a second. This is different – nothing to be afraid of… no bullies or bad guys. Besides I've got Rocky by my side, and God is clearly leading the way on this. It was unbelievable how this was unfolding.

An unexpected concern flashed in my mind: *Is it so clear right now because it's going to be so dark later?*

Gosh, Stacey – just let yourself enjoy this moment. It's okay to enjoy this. Everything's going to be just fine.

Julie hugged me hard just as Rock came walking in the front door. His arms were full with big boxes and little boys.

Yes, I thought,

Everythings going to be just fine...

6

The Road Trip from Hell

"If you do not change direction, you may end up where you were heading."

Lao-Tzu

We were doing it. We were moving. *Finally.*

Everything inside of me would have sighed, but we were too busy. We were actually leaving Southern California, the land of beautiful sunsets, perky boobs, and belly button rings, and heading to a quaint, quirky village in upstate New York. Caleb wanted to "Hep Momma!" But with an infant and a toddler 'helping' packing up took on the form of a circus act. I had kids climbing into boxes, out of boxes, and pooping in boxes. I had friends coming over to actually help pack, clean, and feed us. It was dizzying. My home looked like a pharmaceutical commercial advertising a life that needed Xanax.

As if the kids and cartons weren't enough, Rock and I got it in our minds to let every last person know we were relocating, so we ended up licking envelopes until our tongues were so dry, I could have sworn we were eating sand. We laughed and lisped, sounding like Lucy and Ethel after one of their crazy, hair-brained schemes. My days were about sorting, tossing, and selling my old life to make way for the new life that was coming while trying to work part-time and wrangle two nursing children and still make sure I had quality time with them. Oh, and my husband too.

Yeah. Right.

I needed a spa getaway more than I needed a road trip, but I was excited to get in the minivan with my husband and kids and *on...our...way.* My friend with young kids kept asking me, "Are you sure you want to *drive? All the way?* With the *kids?"*

What? Was I going to leave them somewhere and just take off? Of course we were driving. With the kids. All the way. It was going to be *great.*

I mean, I was prepared. Stocked with blank journals, healthy snacks, and parenting books on CD in tow. I knew it was going to be a bonding time for our family. After having so many conversations and good-byes in our short eight weeks of prepping for our move, I was ready to get on the road and in isolation with my crew. It was time to get reacquainted with them.

On the blank pages of the journals, I imagined Rock and me writing our dreams and goals down before we arrived in New York. I pictured us stopping at state parks across our great nation and picnicking while the kids experienced their first encounter with wild nature. I envisioned the children napping for hours in the car while my husband and I held hands and listened to parenting tips so that we could become extraordinary parents as we drove 3,000 miles in the serenity of the sunsets.

It was going to be magical.

Driving my two little kids across the

Whole

Freakin'

Country...

Oh. My. Glob. What was I thinking?

How could this be God's will? How did I forget how much my children cried on the eight minute drive to Trader Joe's from our home? Or that my husband has a magnetic attraction to McDonad's hamburgers the minute he hears the words '"road trip?"

Or that I would have to visit a restroom every 17 miles since my second son nearly dragged my bladder out in the delivery room?

Oh nooooo... *what did I do?*

We hit every weird weather system imaginable, including hail the size of softballs in New Mexico. We went in the wrong direction for hours (more than once) and ended up driving an average of 250 miles a day. I had only planned for a six-day adventure. At the rate we were going, it would take *forever* to get there.

God, are you kidding me? Really? This is not what I had planned. I had this vision, remember? The happy family driving off into the sunset? The bonding time with my husband and kids? Now all I want to do is leave them all at the next rest stop. This wasn't part of my script.

Juice spilled on the journals. We lived at McDonald's. My children ate the tips of the washable (yet, not so washable) markers.

No one pooped.

No one slept.

Everyone cried at some point, including my husband.

And the cellophane never even made it off the parenting CDs.

By day four, soggy from all the wet weather, we reached El Paso, Texas (which most people can drive to within a long, single day from California and still have time for showers, a Tex Mex dinner, and a good night's sleep). I'd had it. I felt like I was lost in an endless sea called Texas, and everything was on the other side of it.

Where was California? *On the other side.*

New York? *The other other side.*

Where was my sanity? *Dear Lord Jesus, it was on the other flippin' side of Texas.*

I needed somebody to rescue me.

Without much remorse, I probably could have shipped the two little people and one big person off in FedEx boxes to the East while I had my solo 'Thelma and Louise' moment off the edge of a cliff somewhere.

And the only grace I could see was that my husband didn't cut me up into teeny-tiny pieces and leave me in a paper bag on the side of the road.

At one point, I thought, "Let's just give up, stay in Texas, and live here."

We were never going to make it to New York... *alive.*

It was the road trip from hell.

On day eight of our six-day road trip, we crossed into Pennsylvania. I would have cried, but I was too exhausted. Ah, Pennsylvania… we found you! We were so close to New York that I could almost hear Frank Sinatra singing to me, "If I can make it there…"

Geesh. If I could make it there, it'd be a freakin' miracle.

Finally, after 12 hours of driving through a state that seems a lot smaller than Texas – until you actually start driving through it – we pulled out our AAA book and found a hotel in the business district of Harrisburg. With two kids who hadn't eaten dinner, asleep in the car, and a husband who had tuned me out about five states ago, we just needed to *get* there.

I was driving on that rainy night, when a truck got between me and the off-ramp. I couldn't get over fast enough without risking an accident, and completely missed my exit. It would be another 45 minutes around the loop.

That was it.

I was done.

I just couldn't take it anymore.

As I drove in the rain around the city, lost for almost an hour, I was at the point of weeping, "Why, God, why?' Why is this happening? We're just trying to get to New York to serve YOUR people, and I'm going to need to be institutionalized before I get there. I need to know why…"

Our trip was starting to seem like some freakin' biblical epic, but instead of walking around Egypt for 40 years following

Moses, we were going to spend a lifetime driving around the Pennsylvania turnpike.

It was happening again…

That distinct feeling that God was like Lucy with the football – promising that she wouldn't pull it away, leading us to go on this trip, giving us all the signs and signals that would set aside our skepticism and have us pack up our family and move. And I was like Charlie Brown – having all this experience of landing on my back, feeling defeated from my past experiences, but wanting to believe that this time would be different.

This wasn't feeling very different.

I was a whimpering mess when we pulled into the hotel parking lot. I couldn't even look my husband in the eye. The kids were wide awake and rarin' to go. I had no dinner for them, and we were not getting back in that van to search out another fast food extravaganza. I grabbed as many bananas as I could fit between the three fingers that weren't already carrying something else, and we headed to our room for a night of jumping on beds until they were worn out.

Bonus: The added surprise of party people across from our room.

Oh, good. Just what we need…

At some ridiculously ridiculous hour, we finally fell asleep.

Then, what felt like a minute later:

"Momma?" The soft, little hand on my face, rubbing me not-so-gently awake. "Momma?!" The voice got louder and the rubbing harder.

"Wha' honey? You okay?"

"Look! Momma! Sun!"

It had rained for nearly our entire trip. But here we were on Day 9, and it was a sunny Sunday morning. *Oh, thank you, Jesus.* This must be a good sign. I turned to my 2 ½ year old, Caleb, who had finally stopped smooshing my face and said to him, "You love pancakes?" He nodded with wide, happy eyes. "And we're not eating one more lobby bar breakfast." He copied my shaking head and jutted out his 'No way, Jose!' pouty lips. I personally could not face one more hard-boiled egg, packaged Danish, and boxed juice breakfast.

"Let's go find pancakes, Caleb!" He was jumping up and down while I turned to my husband and said, "We'll meet you and Seth downstairs." Then, I dragged myself out of bed.

We went down to the concierge to get directions to the local diner, but Caleb wandered away from me and went into the hotel lobby breakfast bar where all the constipating foods lived. He must have been on automatic pilot. I was just about to call his name when I heard the screaming.

Top of the lungs, ear-piercing, heart-stopping, somebody's-injured-or-seriously-pissed kind of howling.

It was Caleb, and I went running.

I found him standing by the breakfast counter and began furiously searching his body for the owie.

"Oh, he's fine," declared the perky, petite woman in her 50s with short, curly hair. She had the look and confidence reminiscent of Peter Pan. The woman had obviously slept more than I had and was assuring me with one hand waving nonchalantly, "He just tried to touch the coffee pot that somebody left on the edge of the counter, but I told him, 'no' and he got scared."

I comforted my son while 'uh-huh-ing' her.

"He's a cutie! How old is he?" she asked.

"Two and a half." I answered, distractedly.

"What's your name, cutie?" She bent over, her voice full of energy and curiosity, like she was ready to make a friend. I, normally the extrovert, couldn't have been less interested.

"Caleb." I answered dryly. *Do you want to watch him for two hours so I can have a nap and a shower?* I thought.

She kept chirping along, "Oh! I have a grandson named Jackson who is about the same age." On and on she went.

I. Didn't. Care.

I didn't have enough energy to care about my own life, let alone hers. Plus, she was irritating me with how upbeat she was.

Please, just make it all stop and go away, I silently prayed. *Please, if you're a God of compassion, make **her** stop and just go away.*

I was a haggard mess. No make-up, no shower, no sleep, and a daily diet of Big Macs and screaming kids had finally taken its toll. I had officially lost it, and it showed.

Mustering up my last shred of human decency, I gathered my manners, "Look, I'm sorry, I don't mean to be rude, and I really am a good mom. We've just been traveling from California to New York. We're moving to serve a little village of people with our music and honestly, it's been a living, breathing nightmare of a trip. No one is pooping. No one is sleeping..." I'm telling her all of my personal business as she's staring at me, probably afraid I was going to give her the 'how-often-we've-had-sex-report' (don't ask). "My husband is just getting off the elevator right there with my youngest son, Seth." I pointed to the doors. "We'll be there today, if we don't lose our minds before then."

I caught her staring at me after I delivered my depressing monologue. She was so quiet. And pale. As if she'd just seen a ghost

"What's. Your. Name?" She whispered dramatically. I stared at her like she had asked me to solve a math problem.

"Stacey Robbins?" I answered hesitantly, not quite sure after all those days in the car with my kids. She paused and searched my eyes as if I were lying or something.

Slowly and incredulously, she stage-whispered,

"Stacey! It's ME!"

I stared at her some more. She continued.

"Nancy. From Alaska!"

My first thought was,

But I've never been to Alaska.

I was scanning my brain for some past conference I'd spoken at where I might have met this woman before.

Nancy... Nancy... Nancy, from Alaska... who the heck IS this?

I was racking my fast-food-filled, sleep-deprived brain, while she stared at me with wide-eyed anticipation. Then, it hit me.

About a year before, Julie had given me a book of spiritual steps for healing. In the back of the book, there is a phone number to call to sign up with a counselor who can walk you through the steps, every week for a year. The ministry had assigned me a spiritual counselor who I had been talking to every week, right up until we had left for New York. This woman had become a friend to me. She knew the ins-and-outs of my life and cared for me deeply, even though we had never met.

This woman was *Nancy*.

From *Alaska.*

And here she was standing in front of me.

In a town I hadn't planned on stopping in.

In a hotel I hadn't planned on staying in.

In a lobby breakfast bar I hadn't planned on eating in.

She jumped around in a circle clapping her hands like Tigger while I stood there feeling more like Eeyore. She flung herself at me in an unabashed childlike embrace. As I slowly hugged her back, I was inordinately aware of how tall I was next to her. I should have been thinking more profound thoughts like, "Wow, this is incredible — a miracle!" But honestly, I wasn't.

Nancy was beside herself with excitement, but I felt so lukewarm. I couldn't tell if my lack of enthusiasm was from shock or fatigue — or worse — that weird thing inside of me that wouldn't allow me to get excited for fear that the other shoe would drop. I was already asking myself the practical questions: "Why did this happen? What am I supposed to do with this?"

I started doing all the math in my head.

All the wrong turns, the delays, all the meltdowns on the side of the road... all so this moment could take place? *God, I thought you had left me in Texas with two possessed children and a resentful husband while you went to the Bahamas or something. I guess not.*

God had to be doing something. But what? I turned my head mid-hug to see Rock staring at me with exhaustion and bewilderment as he moved toward me from across the room. He raised his eyebrows in that *'What the heck are you doing now, and why is this stranger hugging you?'* sort of way.

Nancy released her clutching hug and energetically flitted from me to the cafe tables where her friends were sitting — to tell them who I was and what had just happened. I was a study in contrast, standing there like an awkward statue trying to explain to Rock what just happened.

I nodded towards her and simply said to Rock, "It's Nancy..."

He stared at me like I had said, "Frogs fly."

I continued, "...from Alaska."

Just about the moment Rock realized who she was, Nancy saw the light bulb go on and came over to hug him too. The man is just about 6'3, so it was like watching a child hug a tree. They were in mid-embrace when I introduced Nancy to Rock and Seth. She had already met Caleb, and there was pretty much nothing she didn't know about me.

Rock glanced to the side and quickly stepped away to stop Caleb who was systematically eating his way through every donut he could reach. Nancy stood in front of me, exhaled, and shook her head, saying over again, "Wow. Wow. Wow."

With a determined finger pointing in my face, she looked at me and said, "Do you know how much He loves you and me, to do this for us?"

I barely blinked. I just stood there. While she would have totally understood my mental ramblings, I didn't know what to say. She knew better than anybody that I was a mix of strong faith and strong doubts – with a lifetime of baggage and blessings that I didn't know how to sort through. I spent most of my time living a life that I thought I should be grateful for but was mostly anxious about.

I had a God I said I believed in but sometimes felt I was on spiritually shaky ground.

How could I say that I believe in this God of love and yet not trust him?

This God of joy and not be happy?

This God of peace and still be anxious?

But maybe this is just what love is — this crazy, manic, back and forth, 'drop you on your head, then give you a miracle' kind of thing. Maybe I was just trying to make sense of it when I should have just accepted that love, even God's love, is nuts.

I just wasn't sure what I knew anymore.

This God up there?

Out there?

In here?

Yeah, He loves me…

I think.

7

Bananas, Cartwheels, and Pancakes, Oh My...

"Follow the yellow brick road."

Glinda, the Good Witch

We were sitting at a small table in the hotel lobby staring at each other. Nancy said, "Wow," every few minutes and shook her head. I kept thinking: Now what? What do we do with this?

"Okay, Nancy, the seas have parted — you don't ask where your shoes are, you just go. So, where are we going?"

"Church!" She said definitively. She slapped her hand on the table to punctuate the decision.

I felt a little deflated. It could be considered a little nervy to feel so blah after having such a remarkable thing happen to you, but I've been known to err on the side of nervy.

Honestly, I think I just wanted something that sounded more exciting and adventurous than going to church. I wanted her to say something clarifying in a deep voice, possibly a British accent (for effect). It could start with something like, "Ahem... attention! The reason God brought me here was to give you this important message for your life..." followed by clear instructions to climb a mountain then trudge through a raging creek as we embarked on some God-scavenger hunt for the Holy Grail or whatever it was we were supposed to find. After eight days of sitting in a car, I wasn't really thinking, *Oh goody! Let's go sit for a couple of hours in a church and hope that God does something and that I don't miss it.*

If it were simply a case of going anywhere and guessing, couldn't God have spoken to us at Denny's over a Grand Slam breakfast special with all the pancakes a talkative two-year-old could hold? Yet, I was torn. A part of me thought God would be much happier if I were in church. And maybe if He were happier, He'd be more likely to speak something to me. It's not like I didn't have evidence to the contrary, because I did. In the Bible, I saw that God communicated through a burning bush, a cloud, a donkey… if He did all that stuff then, why couldn't He talk to me at Denny's? What was so impossible about that? It was a fair question, but my theology of formulas had worn a deep groove. I didn't want to take any chances.

It was what she said next that piqued my interest. "Stacey, I came out here last-minute to hear this man speak at this church conference for the last four days. He's been amazing, and he's been talking about people like you all week. I think his message is for you! He's speaking this morning. I think I'm supposed to take you there."

See, she had me right there. I had no idea what she meant by 'people like me,' but I was hooked by thinking that someone knew more about me in some special way. And I was more than curious to see if God was going to give me some big 'aha!' that would take away all this inner restlessness and spiritual anxiety that was plaguing me. I desperately needed that.

I just kinda hoped it wasn't going to be one of those bombastic crusade type of events.

Like most people in America, I've seen the pastors on TV in white designer suits banging on their Bibles or on someone's forehead. I was extremely skeptical about all the hype and people screaming the name of God like it was a two-syllable word. Anything resembling a church show was a complete turn-off to me. And yet, I admit there was some innocent hope inside of me that caused me to pause sometimes before changing the channel. I would sit on the edge of the couch and scan the TV screen, searching for some shred of evidence that it might be real. And maybe some of it was, but more often than not, it made my stomach turn at the thought of people being tricked and taken advantage of in the name of God.

I had come all this way, and this unbelievable encounter had just occurred. How could I not go over and check it out, no matter what shape or style the messenger was? I mean, seriously, that German missionary lady wasn't what I expected either...

Maybe this is the answer I've been searching for. Maybe peace is waiting there for me and I just have to go get it.

So, off we went. With me battling the 'I'm a selfish-mom' guilt over not keeping the pancake promise to my son just so I could go down another rabbit hole after spiritual peace. I grabbed cranky kids, a wary husband, and another slew of bananas, and in the shockingly normal afterglow of the miraculous, we headed off to church.

We sat through a music segment that I thought would never end. I like music and all, but this was endless. *Do I do this to people? Make them sit through music they don't really want to hear, longer than they want to hear it?* To distract myself from having to face the answer, I scoured the red-carpeted room for any possible signs from God.

Nothing.

I alternated my scoping with bowing my head and praying, *God, will you please let the music end so that we can get on with it?* Ugh. Everything in me wanted to do my usual 'slip out to the ladies room when I'm bored' routine but I was afraid to leave. I didn't want to miss God doing a cartwheel or something in the middle of the service, just because I had the patience of a gnat.

And, that nagging thing in me kept coming to the surface: Wanting to be a good girl. And good girls stayed, even if they were bored. Actually, really good girls wouldn't have gotten bored at church in the first place.

Good girls were *always…*

Always helpful

Always said, "Yes."

Yes, I'll help with the kids in the nursery.

Yes, I'll bring a meal to the potluck.

Yes, I'll stay late and rehearse the music set one more time!

And even,

Yes, you can count on me being silent when things don't make sense to me

And

Yes you can hurt me and I won't do a damn thing about it.

I was spent from the constant activity from all of my 'yes's'. But more than that, I was exhausted from what was driving me to say yes. I was afraid to slow down, to say, "No"... to disappoint God. Anybody who's ever read the Old Testament knows what a disappointed God does...

(read: ground opening, storms raging, people dying.)

No matter how I felt and no matter all the hang-ups behind those feelings, I didn't come all this way to miss it, whatever 'it' was, so...I stayed put.

And then, finally, he stepped onto the stage.

Ooooh! Yay! Excited, I sat up, pen and paper in hand, feeling like the pageant spotlight was shining right on me. I was ready to receive the answer I was here for.

While I was gearing up, Nancy's shoulders fell slightly.

What now?

The adrenaline rushing through my body honed in on the smallest change in Nancy's demeanor. She shook her head. This wasn't the 'special' guy from out of town, the one who'd have the special message just for special, ol' me. Nope. Nancy was mistaken. Come to find out, that guy had already left town.

Crap.

I wanted to grab the nearest usher by his lapels, pull him right up to my face and yell, "Are you kidding me? Do I not look frazzled enough with all the hell I've been through?"

It's like I missed the turnpike exit all over again.

Breathe, Stacey. Breathe.

I glanced over at Nancy. She had already bounced back, and with the pat of her hand was trying to encourage me that it was perfect just the way it was. It's hard to have that kind of faith when you're tired and you want something to be the way you thought it should be, instead of the way it is.

I held her hand, and she squeezed it. It *was* truly incredible that she and I had 'run into' each other in such an extraordinary encounter.

Seriously, I can't find my husband in the same grocery store where I plan to meet him, and here, Nancy and I had somehow found each other.

Wow, indeed.

There had to be a reason, and I wanted to hear it. Hopefully this wouldn't be the once-a-year money drive for the church's multi-purpose room or something.

Sigh.

God, why do I feel so resentful and grateful instead of just grateful? How can I just live in the grateful part of this whole thing? Before I had time for God to answer, the speaker began.

His message was on 'rest.'

How important rest is.

How sacred rest is.

How beautiful rest is.

Rest.

Really?

You're kidding me…

I was in the middle of a move, barely surviving the road trip from Hell, going to a new community with new people who expected us to serve them and meet their needs because that's what we said we would do. Up ahead was unpacking boxes, getting kids situated, starting a new job, making new friends.

And all the while, there were these other rumblings underneath it all that I just couldn't ignore:

My own inner voice calling me to 'be still' and the odd German lady confirming that message.

Nancy from Alaska, at just the right place and time. And then, today, this message of rest.

I honestly didn't know what to do with it all.

I just wanted to get to New York and start this wonderful new peaceful life I'd been imagining for years. I'd been waiting a long time, and I had a lot to do.

Even though it had been stalking me for so many years, and in so many ways, 'Rest' was definitely *not* on my to-do list.

8

Parables from the Kitchen: Life and Other Four-Letter Words

"It's not true that life is one damn thing after another; it is one damn thing over and over."

Edna St. Vincent Millay

It was the drum that wouldn't stop beating, and I had been hearing it relentlessly in the last couple of years, even before the 'be still' thing. There was this moment when I was pregnant with Seth that this message seemed to flow through me. I was sitting at my OB appointment, and my doctor was epidemically late, so I started bringing a book to every appointment. This time it was *Traveling Light for Mothers* by Max Lucado. Engrossed and in deep concentration on each word, I suddenly became inspired, quickly flipping to the blank extra pages in the back of the book. I grabbed the pen with the pharmaceutical name on it from the nurse's station and began to channel these words:

REST is pruning back our work so that our growth may be more productive.

REST says:

I TRUST

that I'm not in control of the world.

But it also says I BELIEVE

that my job,

calling,

LIFE

is so important that I need to do what's best,

And what's best is to rest.

Example: When I get a nice, quality candle, it directs me to cut the wick. I never want to cut the wick. I like the long wick. It makes me feel better, like there's more. Apparently, I don't trust that the people who made the candle know what they're talking about.

Hello!

Listen to that.

The PEOPLE who MADE the candle don't know better?! I know better?

What makes me the authority?

Oh, I'm not the authority.

Just like when God says to REST. He knows better; He knows what I need.

Because He made me.

It was such a clear spiritual message that came spontaneously through me but was also completely un-relatable to my life.

Rest isn't even on the list of most moms I know. Because rest is a joke if you have kids, especially if you have busy kids like my toddler boys. Energetic, jumping up and down off the furniture, swinging from the chandeliers, super bright, verbal boys. I tell people as we're whizzing by in a blur, "Don't mind us. We're just living life at the speed of Caleb…" as my voice trails off in the distance.

Rest is a joke if you're a Type A personality.
Rest is a joke if you have unconfessed control issues.
(Rest is a joke if you have *confessed* control issues.)
Rest is a joke if you've just moved cross-country.

Rest is a joke if you have ugly wallpaper that makes you want to cry and drop everything else until it's completely peeled off. All 7 layers of it.

Followed by bubblegum pink paint underneath.

I wish I were kidding but I'm not.

In fact, I was trying to find the punchline for this joke.

How was I going to rest when people in our new village were ready for me to jump in and start working? But even more, how was I going to rest when I had this thing inside of me driving me to keep going… 'or else?' Even though I knew better and was getting all of these cosmic messages, it wasn't an easy hamster wheel to exit. Plus, we glorify 'busy' all the time in our performance-oriented Western culture, and we use rest as a reward for our work instead of as an essential element of our design.

We say things like:

*When I have a secure job… When my stocks are up… When my weight is down… When my kids stop nursing, are potty-trained, go to school, finish school, find a job, find a wife, have their kids… **then,** I'll be able to rest.*

We all have justifications for why we're not slowing down. I hear them all the time. I even asked at a women's conference one weekend, "What are you all waiting for?" One dry, monotone voice broke through the crowd, "For my mother-in-law to die."

And there you go.

Since there will always be something we're waiting for, there'll always be something driving us.

How many stories do we hear about people who live miserably in a job they hate, marking the Xs on their calendar as if they're in prison just waiting to be released, only to lose their health or their loved one when they finally retire? And still, like rats in a maze, we keep thinking we'll rest and find blissful inner peace when some external goal is finally achieved.

"When…"

It's such a lie because we can keep creating new projects and deadlines that haven't been met until we breathe our very last.

Even though I had glimpses of how I was living in that lie, I didn't know how to stop. I had so many plates spinning between family, work, church, and moving, that I didn't know how I could keep everything going and rest at the same time. And the thing is this: They were all good things.

97

Noble pursuits. It's not like I had this extra hobby of robbing banks or stripping at some skanky bar (oh, dear Lord, no – keep that cellulite to yourself, Stacey!) and if I'd just cut them out of my life, I would have all this free time. It wasn't like that.

My life was 'good.'

The challenge to living your life so full of good things is that people rarely ever call you on it. How often does someone who's benefiting from our busyness walk up to us and say, "Oh, Darling, you have *got* to slow down! We are running way too efficiently and smoothly because of all you're doing. We need you to stop and take real good care of yourself. Don't worry your pretty little head if we fall apart at the seams – you just need your *rest.*"

Nope. Folks don't do that. It's usually the exact opposite.

"Oh I know that you're already so, so busy but you're the only person who could handle something this sensitive. Do you have a few minutes to fit this in?"

We hail busy people as heroes in our culture. I saw it in my church experience too. It seemed that the person who did the most was the most revered. I kept amending my already crazy theology as I observed this: If doing more equals good girl, then doing less must equal bad.

How do I listen to this 'rest' message from God and not be seen as some lazy, bad girl to my church?

I'd heard of a church near my house where the pastor said something like, "If you're in that chair and you're not serving, you can get up and leave right now and give that chair to someone who *will* serve." Youch. That was an overt, and may I add, crappy way of saying it. But I'll tell you, I kept hearing the undercurrent of that message come through at almost every church I went to, and it was always linked up with God's approval or disapproval. That was the part that was screwing me up in my head.

Rest was definitely not part of the vernacular of my culture and it showed. I was fried – like that last little crispy French fry stuck in the bottom corner of the fast food bag. But I still didn't know how to rest.

And at every turn, Someone was clearly trying to get my attention.

"Rock! Honey? Somebody's at the door!"

Nothing.

"Rocky?"

The Man wasn't answering. Maybe he was with the kids out exploring the little shed with the random headboard and life-sized Santa Claus light-up plastic statue left by the last owner, which, by the way, scared the ever-loving poop out of me when I walked into the shed for the first time in the pitch dark.

"Forget it. I'll get it," I said to myself as I finished washing a dish in my kitchen with the butt-ugly wallpaper.

I opened the door to find a very smiley, more than middle-aged man with a huge, speckled dog at his side.

"Hi there, new neighbor!" He was warm and affable with his greeting, and I felt, for some strange reason, like I was seeing an old friend. I'm Ed, from across the street." He pointed over to the blue-and-white Victorian with the wraparound porch, "and this here is Freckles, The Wonder Dog."

I smiled and said, "Hi, Ed from across the street, and hello, Freckles, the Wonder Dog. I'm Stacey. To what do I owe this pleasure?"

"Well, Stace..." The fact that he called me by one of my nicknames right off the bat made me smile even more, "I'm just here to tell you that it's time to boil the water."

My brow furrowed, "Huh?"

"Well, you see, this here town thought it would be best to do the piping underneath the ground in the 'cost-effective' way (read: cheap), and when it rains or snows, the dirt seeps into the water in the pipes and makes it turbid..."

(Note to self: when Ed leaves, look up the definition of turbid).

"...the fire department always puts up a sign telling us when to do it, but I figured since you're new and you're prolly holed-up here gettin' situated, you didn't see it."

He figured right, so I nodded. He started to leave, "So wait, Ed. I've got to boil the water before I drink it?"

"Yup," he turned and confirmed it with his deadpan look, "And then, skim it."

Whoa whoa whoa...

"Did you say boil it *and* skim it?" I shook my head in a 'no' direction, trying to will his answer that way.

"Yup. There's this film that you'll get on top after it boils, and you're not gonna wanna drink that, so s'best to skim it."

Ugh.

I'm not sure if I rolled my eyes, but Ed's just twinkled that kind, fatherly way that says he knows the inside joke to life. He and Freckles turned and headed down the driveway.

"Nice to meet you, Ed! Thanks for letting me know...I think," I called to him.

"Good to meet you, too, Stace. You let me and Freckles know if you guys need anything, okay?"

"You got it, Ed. Will do!"

I closed the door and leaned against it. You have got to be kidding me. Not after all the hell it took to get here and all the work we've got to do. I've got two kids in diapers. *God, you're not going to make me boil water like we're on some 'Little House on the Prairie' episode gone bad, are you? This is America, for Pete's sake; not some third world country.*

I went back into the kitchen, not believing Ed. It was time to make dinner, so I ran the water and put the pot for spaghetti under the spigot. *He's crazy. This looks fine. Perfectly clear running water.* I convinced myself that Ed must be the sidekick to Freckles, The Wonder Dog, instead of the other way around. I turned off the water and crossed the room to turn on the stove. The thing was being persnickety and wouldn't light at first, but by the third try, the whoosh sound of the flame rose up. I turned back and saw it before I reached the sink. The pot in the sink was filled three quarters of the way up with the most disgusting brown water I had ever seen. I just stood and stared.

I groaned when it hit me.

That's me.

That freakin' water is me...

Running and looking fine. Helping others, raising my family, running a music business with my husband, speaking at events, learning how to homeschool my kids, moving cross-country... I looked good at a zillion miles an hour as I flew by you in a blur, but man, when I slowed down on the outside, this anxiety started revving up on the inside. Busyness was the drug for my anxiety. No wonder resting wasn't my favorite thing in the world.

My spiritual water was a murky mess: dark, dirty, and troubled. But with what?

What's the deal, God? I was just looking to make spaghetti over here... I wasn't looking for a parable.

I pulled a chair from the dining room into the middle of the kitchen where I was having this revelation about the brown water and me.

"Okay, God. What's up?"

And just then a question appeared: *Stacey, do you trust my love?*

Was that me asking, or was it God? I didn't hear it as much as I felt it. I knew something was asking me. And if it was God, then why would He ask a question He already knew the answer to?

I answered anyway. "Not in all ways. Not in all times." I paused, afraid to ask the next question, "Does that mean not at all, Lord?"

Silence.

More silence.

This wasn't looking good for me. I started to squirm.

In the wake of that confession and the awkward silence, I immediately wanted to fix it. I was so embarrassed. I did my typical response with God, rolling up my sleeves and rubbing my hands together. *Okay, God. Here we go. Let's fix it. Right now. What do we do? Let's get to work!*

Imagine what it would sound like if God gently shook his head in a *No, no, no* kind of way. It's as if He were saying to me, "You don't get it. You're not going to do anything. I'm going to do it. You just rest."

Normally, I was really good at applying more spiritual elbow grease to get the job done. But apparently old methods weren't going to cut it now.

'Rest' was quickly becoming my new four-letter word.

9

Will the Real God Please Stand Up (And Stop Scaring the Hell Out of Me)

"To me, clowns aren't funny. In fact, they're kind of scary. I've wondered where this started and I think it goes back to the time I went to the circus, and a clown killed my dad."

Jack Handy

Honestly, I'm not a very good patient. When I was 16, I had all four of my impacted wisdom teeth removed. I was instructed to sip broth and drink milkshakes. Instead, a few hours after my surgery, I ate a chewy, delicious New York bagel with cream cheese and almost ripped out all of my stitches. My mother wanted to strangle me.

When I was 17, I found out I had mono. I breezed right past the doctor's advice to take it real easy and sleep a lot; there could be a possible negative effect on my spleen, and blah, blah, blah…

Instead I came home, did an aerobics workout, and then cleaned the already clean house from head-to-toe in my typical extreme way.

So when the 'rest' message kept hitting me right and left, I handled it in like fashion. Like a suggestion for the other mere mortals…I grabbed my Bible, my journal, and a stack of dusty unread devotionals that I had collected over the previous years, and found my way to the chair on the back porch. Surrounded by books on my left and my Bible on my right, I had a couple of inches of space on my lap for my journal and pen. I was ready for 'rest.' Rarin' to rest. But as I started pouring over the pages, something started niggling at me. I found myself having to reread the same lines over and over and over again. My mind was bothered.

You know when you feel like someone is staring at you? I couldn't shake that sense.

I tilted my head back so I could see up to wherever heaven is and asked, "Too much?"

Does God sigh with exasperation? I think I heard it in the wind that day. I'm pretty sure He rolled His eyes too. I sheepishly closed everything and set it all aside.

Okay God. I can do this.

'Rest.'

I've got this!

So, I started talking, *"Do you want me to sing to you? Is there something you want to say to me or that I should say to you? Is there someone you want me to pray for? Are you okay that I'm sitting, or should I be kneeling? Is this right? Am I doing it right? Are we done yet? Ummmm, how exactly will I know when we're done?"*

That's when these words passed through my head in the most holy and loving way,

Stop, Stacey.

Just.

Stop.

Talking.

A picture appeared in my mind's eye: A surgeon, a nurse, and a patient lying on an operating table. And in that way that only happens in dreams or imaginations, I had a deep and wordless understanding in the instant that it came to my mind. God was the surgeon. He knew what was wrong and how to fix it. Jesus was the nurse. He was going to be taking care of supporting The Surgeon's work. And The Spirit was the anesthesiologist. It was going to knock me out and monitor me so that I could be in those grace-filled depths of rest while the work was done.

And me? I was the patient. My big job was to show up, shut up, and be still. I got the message and felt strangely comforted, the way you do when anesthesia starts hitting you. Yet within this dreamy state, I was also still very aware of my concern.

_____

In my mind, God had never really been a 'surgeon.' I had a few strong images of Him, but surgeon was never one of them. He was the policeman I never noticed until I did something wrong, and when I did, suddenly there were blaring sirens and tickets being thrown at me. With this policeman god, I did not pass go, and I did not go straight to jail when I screwed up. Nope, I just went straight to Hell.

Sometimes he was the Santa Claus god with a touch of Zeus.

His whole gig was to check and see if I was naughty or nice.

If I was a good girl and said "yes" all the time, I would be rewarded with the sexy butt, car with leather seats, and the guys who would buy me diamonds. But if I was naughty, well, I would get punished with the big butt with the granny panties, the cloth interior in my car, and guys who needed me to bail them out of jail. The lightning bolts could be thrown at me in the form of appendicitis, my parents divorcing, or a flat tire just as I got that check for $50 from Aunt Millie for my birthday. Just so I knew who was in charge and who was boss and how much I had pissed him off.

He was my Santa Zeus god.

Then, there was this third identity in my unholy trinity: This one was just the opposite of the other two micromanaging gods. This was my Bette Midler god. And like her famed song proclaimed, "God is watching us… God is watching us… God is watching us… from a distance." I could picture that god too – that removed god. Only if I lived in a cave and was draped in a cloth meditating all day in some Zen kind of way would God even come close. The rest of the time, he was this out there, not here kind of god.

That far away god wasn't really my main concern because he was the most benign of the three. I was more aware of the easily and chronically disappointed god, the one who was on his last nerve with humanity – on the verge of destroying earth, and sending everyone to The Lake of Fire. I felt like we had established the terms of the relationship: he gets to do whatever he wants, whenever he wants, and however he wants. And I? Well, I get to walk on eggshells.

All of these misconceptions kept me paralyzed on one hand and running like a crazy person on the other. It was like living in an abusive relationship where the abuser threatens to kill you if you try to leave, but you know you'll live a tormented life if you stay.

This Franken-god I served was looking more and more like a terrorist…

Or maybe,

Something worse.

10

The Devil Wears Ann Taylor

"Naturally we would prefer seven epiphanies a day and an earth not so apparently devoid of angels."

Jim Harrison

We were still so new to each other.

Kathryn and I met four years before at an interfaith conference in Midland, Texas. We were on day three of a four-day event filled with main sessions, breakout groups, meet and greets, and training opportunities – all powered by donuts, caffeine, extroverts, and the Holy Spirit.

I was the lone music leader, and she was in the sea of hundreds of spiritual leaders from different faiths across the country – all there to experience unity in song and prayer. Pastor James, the conference leader, a graying man in his 60s, stood at the front to give next-day instructions and to dismiss everyone with the final prayer.

"This service is ended. Let us go out to love and serve the Lord." And the crowd answered the traditional response: "Thanks be to God!" dispersing to the lobby for coffee and conversations.

I was used to a variety of people who came up to talk at the end of the day: The bubbly Southern Pentacostal women excited to share what God was showing them during the conference; the jovial West Coast pastors relaxed in their Hawaiian shirts and Dockers giving me big hugs to thank me for my music; the priests from the North East with their strong accents and warm eyes who loved knowing I was raised Catholic… and so many more. This convergence of cultures and faiths all meeting in one room warmed me and made me feel part of a bigger whole.

That's when I met Kathryn. She stood, waiting patiently in the dimly lit sanctuary while the usual afterglow stragglers stayed behind in meditation. Slowly, and with measured steps, she moved toward me. She was tiny in stature, her jet-black hair elegantly grayed in just the right places, swept behind her ear, revealing tasteful pearl earrings. She was lovely and put-together, with an air of mystery around her. If I had not seen the clerical collar, I could have easily pictured her sipping bisque off a silver spoon at a country club for a ladies luncheon.

So it surprised me that someone so seemingly demure would grasp my arm – a stranger's arm, no less – with such intensity as she did. Lifting her chin in a regal way, she moved in closer.

"Stacey, your music is transcendent… *otherworldly.*" She closed her eyes and nodded, affirming her own words. "I sense the Lord saying that we will work together one day – that God is going to use you for great things… and I'm supposed to help you to accomplish them."

I stared. Such bold statements right out the gate following her compliment. While I was used to people who were known as 'prophetic' coming up to me and sharing thoughts about how God was going to use me for His work or what not, there was something different about her. Her gaze and her words drew me in, and I found myself falling under the spell of her spirituality. She continued:

"You know, I sense that you are someone who has always heard from God, even in the miserable times." I found myself nodding even though a part of me wanted to have more self-restraint around this stranger. "And you have always known there was something of greatness you were going to do with your life..." She closed her eyes and paused to breathe in more inspiration.

I watched her face and listened to her words – she seemed so connected to God, sharing the vision of me that I couldn't always see due to the clouding insecurities that would swell within me. It compelled me to let down my guard.

The intensity of the moment broke when the custodial staff rolled in the heavy cart, "I'm so sorry. How rude of me... my name is Kathryn." I had read it on her nametag but we just hadn't taken the moment to formally introduce ourselves. She held out her delicate hand with slim fingers, the strength of which surprised me when she shook my hand. "Reverend Kathryn Winters from the United Methodist Church in Dobbs Ferry, New York. And, of course, I know you and your music well from the last few days. It's been just lovely, Stacey." She bowed slightly in acknowledgement, and I nodded my thanks. She motioned toward the foyer and asked, "May we have a few more minutes out in the lobby?"

I smiled and nodded again, "Sure... that'd be nice. Let me just grab my stuff..."

I picked up my guitar, music, and purse in a bit of a haze while she waited. Once there, we chatted about her grown children and that no, I didn't have any... not yet, at least. She nodded and closed her eyes in an almost prayerful way. I grabbed a cup of coffee and noticed her taking an English Tea bag out of her purse while she shared some of the bits of her ministry background, where she had traveled in Europe (she loved England the most), and how she had landed at this particular conference. Her mannerisms and lyrical voice were captivating. I enjoyed our time together which we ended by exchanging contact information with a promise to stay in touch.

Our long-distance relationship continued after the conference – phone calls and emails filled with Kathyrn sharing about how she wanted to strengthen the weaker areas of the church and pursue her ministry dreams. I admit I felt at times during our calls that I was listening in on the middle of a conversation – like I should have known more than I actually did and was trying desperately to catch up. "Oh, and you know Mitzy is definitely nearing the other side of life, so we shall escort her triumphantly back home." I didn't want to risk asking who Mitzy was as it could well have been her cat, her car, her organist, or her mother. I had no idea since she had never mentioned Mitzy before, and in light of the seriousness of the content, I felt foolish asking, "Who's Mitzy?"

It wasn't just content; it was style too.

Though she was American, she would take on something of an Old English way of speaking that left me scratching my head. By the time I caught onto the style, I had missed the content of what she was saying. No matter how fuzzy some parts of our conversations seemed to me, one thing was always clear — she thought I was going to be part of her future.

But life moved on, and after having my two boys in less than two years, I lost touch with a segment of my life outside of my Orange County bubble – which meant I lost touch with Kathryn too – until I got that out-of-the-blue email from her, "Stacey," I could hear her voice in my head even though Rock was reading it to me from the next room, "The Spirit of the Lord has put it upon my heart to invite you to join us at our little church in the North East...." She was asking us to bring our music and messages, as well as a kids' program, to her community. And even though I didn't know much about her specific denomination, she welcomed all of us and was eager to teach me.

And now, after all this time and conversation, we were finally on the same coast, in the same room, staring at each other. Which was not the same as a long-distance relationship.

"Now, Stacey, these people are not like us. They are, well...." Kathryn smoothed a wrinkle that didn't exist on her Ann Taylor slacks and with the back of her hand brushed away an invisible hair from her cheek. She was petite, trim, and coiffed in that understated, stately New England manner. Her skin was porcelain and polished, without a stitch of make-up, making her appear much younger than her 60-something years. There was not an ounce of cleavage or leg showing, yet she was the picture of demure femininity. She belonged to that distinct group of mature women who wear tasteful sapphires for their wedding rings, plant their own gardens, and will split a salad with you at lunch while they have millions in the bank. She must have studied dance in her youth, because every move she made was choreographed to accentuate a point.

She cleared her throat, brought her hands up to her chest in a praying position, and closed her eyes. I heard the nervous 'clicking' from a pen and realized it was mine, so I stopped. After a deep breath, she intertwined her fingers and brought them to her lap.

Kathryn started over, "These people are from a different culture than we are, Stacey..."

Her voice had a condescending ring to it, "...untraveled in the global sense and inexperienced in the matters of the Spirit. *You* understand." Her hand gestured toward me in a complimentary kind of way, but it was awkward. If I acknowledged the compliment, I would at the same time be agreeing that the congregation was the East Coast version of the Beverly Hillbillies.

"Hmmm..." was my non-committal offering. She waited with an expectant look for confirmation, but I bowed my head toward the pad on my lap, pretending to make a note. *Ugh. In my next life I want to be one of those brave people who stand up for what's right all the time.* I noticed my toes pointing slightly in toward each other, something I'd done ever since I was a child whenever I got uncomfortable. She went on defending her position.

"I mean, the people are clearly troubled by a Spirit of Insanity... Oh, and please, let's not forget Gertrude and Rich – they have been attending for 50 years. That woman is controlled by a foul, foul, spirit, Stacey." She donned a strident, elderly voice mimicking Gertrude's, "That's not how we do communion, Kathryn! That's not how we set the altar, Kathryn!''

She then returned back to her own exasperated voice, "So contentious! And the board – pfft... well..." her voice turned in a split-second to a tone that was overly kind and yet completely void of kindness, "Stacey, I can't really blame them. They have had no good leadership for years. That's why the Lord brought me, and I brought you." I lifted my gaze back up to meet hers. I had been staring at her mouth and caught sight of the flush that was creeping up her neck with every new animated story, "This isn't going to be easy, but it's our mission so…" She lit up with excitement, "Let's do something powerful for Christ and lead the way!"

She smiled determinedly, punching her fist down on the leather binder – something I would come to know as her signature move to drive the point home.

I had never seen this side of her. Sure, I had been in many church council and leadership meetings at churches prior where we, as a staff, had the opportunity to let down our guard and talk shop about the cranky usher or the persnickety parishioner who was irritating us. It was a relief to be able to share about things that were driving us nuts. Still, I always felt badly afterwards, like I needed to shower and cleanse myself for engaging in the parts that were gossip. I'd make a renewed commitment to not join in the next time, but when I caved, I was angry at myself for taking part and not speaking up for what I thought was right.

But this conversation with Kathryn had a different air about it. It was shocking to sit across from someone who could wear a collar and manage to insult everybody – from the former leadership to the current congregation – in one fell swoop (all with a smile on her face as if she were handing out candy on Halloween).

Nevertheless, I decided that giving her the benefit of the doubt was probably best. After all, I didn't know them like she did. I didn't have to deal with their alleged idiosyncrasies like she had. And, really, Kathryn and I were like newlyweds, having just tied the knot after being drawn to each other for so many good reasons. Now, in our honeymoon phase, we would each be getting to know the not-so-beautiful stuff that you learn when you start living life together. You just have to keep reminding yourself why you came together in the first place.

Right?

—————————————

Those first few months flew by. Though Rock had never lived on the East Coast, the new autumn chill brought me immediately back to memories of high school football games from my youth. Caleb and Seth were learning the traditions of raking, piling, and jumping into leaves while Rock and I unpacked remaining boxes and peeled endless layers of wallpaper.

We were still engaged in meetings aimed at introducing us to the religious community, to the neighbors, and to the rhythms of the church. Every moment seemed to be filled. No wonder summertime and mosquitoes had whizzed by in such a blur.

It was the night of the mid-week prayer meeting. The warm, whooshing heat from the vents in the old sanctuary was a comfort from the cold outside. The small church was lit with candles on the altar, and the smell of incense filled the room. I sat in the back pew and let myself breathe in the memories from my past.

I could see it as if it were yesterday, my little sisters and I, kneeling in the front row of our church, watching wide-eyed, trying not to gag as the priest walked by with the little smoking incense ball swinging from the chain.

We'd look at each other,

Then look at the ball,

Then back at each other again, trying to hold our breath as long as we could while the priest would pass.

But the inevitable would happen. One of us would be the first to get the watery eyes and the flushed cheeks from trying to not explode or burst out in laughter...or BOTH. Soon the gasping and coughing would start, and that was it. Next thing you know, all three of us were laughing on the floor by the kneelers. We knew the grown-ups were mad but we couldn't help it. When you're a kid, incense is like spiritual tear gas.

The irreverent sound of a nose honking into a handkerchief broke the nostalgic moment. I glanced around the small sanctuary to see who it was.

It was Jerry, with the gray, prickly chin stubble and oversized ears that turned red when he was too warm or too cold, sitting there, wiping his nose with the back of his hand.

Oh dear Lord, please let me drink from the communion cup before he does.

A few pews back, there were Gina and her mother, Donna, sitting with their friend Maria. Gina was like her mother, Donna, who was tall and solid framed. They moved slowly and deliberately when they walked about the church and town. Gina had her red hair in a ponytail, and her mother's was like a red cotton puff, teased so much that it was practically see through. Maria was Donna's best friend, short and round with dark hair and dark eyes that glimmered and shifted back and forth. They seemed to search you like the beam of a flashlight scanning for someone lost in the woods. While Donna would glide slowly about and speak just the same, Maria would flit about with short shuffles and speak so quickly with such a thick New York accent, you'd have to ask her to repeat herself a few times in each conversion. Though they appeared an odd couple at first glance, they were a solid pair of friends who considered each other family, weathering it all throughout the decades. And no matter what, they would always come out stronger together and with God.

And on the groom's side of the church, there was Allen, a middle-aged real estate developer with a somewhat round and regal-looking face, who had a passion for wearing pullover vests with his dress shirts and suit pants, while his father, Martin, a retired business mogul in his 80s with a drawn face, bought his slacks and white collared shirts at Walmart and slept through the entire service. They were the ones Kathryn would roll her eyes about in our meetings and refer to as "The Stingy Millionaires."

This is just how it seemed to be for this small church – these faithful few who'd come out for the prayer meetings and healing nights, silent and scattered among the shiny wooden pews of the candle-lit sanctuary. It made the 25 people who attended Sunday mornings seem downright grand. Meanwhile, the Catholic church down the way boasted 1500 members with standing room-only masses, and the Baptist church a little further down had a very active, happy, non-drinking community of 300.

And while I didn't want to compare numbers from one church to another, I couldn't help but notice the difference.

The mid-week service had begun. Kathryn was on one side of the altar in her proper vestments and white collar, and I was on the other side, standing behind the music keyboard. The large marble table, swathed in a sacred cloth runner with the cross on it, was between us.

"Let us begin with a prayer to our Lord, Jesus Christ." She called in a majestic voice, opening her arms to all eight of us in the near-empty little church. We bowed our heads.

That's when I heard the sobbing.

I glanced up to see it was the young woman, Gina – Donna's daughter – a newlywed who had recently become pregnant. We had started a friendship when we came to visit that first snowy January and were glad to be one of the four younger couples in the church of mostly 60 to 80 year-olds. Though she and her parents and her grandparents had all been part of the congregation for many years – and had stayed well beyond the revolving door of many pastors – she and her family were "not like Kathryn" and, therefore, were barely tolerated by their own new minister.

Gina was inconsolable, with her head buried in her mother's bosom. But Kathryn kept ignoring her, ending the prayer and reading the scriptures louder and louder above the cries. I stood at the keyboard in shock. *Can't she call the girl forward? Does she really have to wait for the part of the service when we take prayer requests? There are only six people out there, for God's sake!*

I looked for a pause in between Kathyrn's words and called to the young woman, "Please, Gina, come up here... tell us what's going on." Kathryn had given me permission to step in when we first arrived, "You are a peer and a partner, Stacey. God has given you authority, and I invite you to use it." But from the fire that flashed in Kathryn's eyes at this moment, I could see those rights being quickly rescinded.

Donna took one arm of her inconsolable daughter, and Donna's friend Maria took Gina's other arm as they helped Gina walk each achingly slow step down the short aisle. Kathryn composed herself quickly, nodded, and put on her concerned face, beckoning them with her hand as if it were her idea to bring them up. But when she went to get the holy water, she turned in my direction and rolled her eyes as if to say, 'Those people...'

Gina collapsed on the padded kneeler at the foot of the altar. Tears streamed down her face, which seemed paler to me, even in the dark sanctuary, while her mom held her in her arms, "I think... I'm losing... my baby." She barely got the words out between sobs. Kathryn nodded and furrowed her brow. She held her hand over the head of the distraught parishioner, prayed a lofty, sing-song-y type of prayer, and seemed peculiarly lost in bliss. It reminded me of those horror movies where some demented woman is killing a cat and singing a nursery rhyme at the same time. It sent shivers through my body and a sick turn to my stomach.

I blinked hard to erase the image while Kathryn put the holy water on the girl's forehead in the sign of the cross. When the service ended, Kathryn was livid, pacing in the empty church with her arms crossed. The clicking of her sensible, designer heels, echoed in the rafters.

"Can you believe those two – catering to Gina? They're all *ridiculous!*" She waved her hand in the air to include 'all' of them. "She didn't *lose* that baby. They all just support each other's melodrama." She waved her hand again. I guess this was going to be the 'all' hand gesture from now on, so I took note. "Stacey, this is what happens in small towns like this. People have nothing better to do than create soap operas." She seethed with every word.

"Kathryn, really? You really think that she's pretending?" I asked.

"Of course she is," she hissed. "They're *ridiculous*. These people are not in their right minds here." She turned on her heel, past the portrait of Jesus, toward the back room to remove her vestments.

When I walked home that night, I noticed a few of the porch lights were on down the tree-lined street. It seemed warm and safe inside of those homes. I wanted to slip inside there and take away the chill I felt inside from what I had just seen.

Though the night sky was clear, grief hung on me like a heavy cloud, and it hadn't lifted at all by the time I walked in the door. Rock was sitting at the table with the computer when he saw my face.

"Honey? What's wrong?" his voice filled with concern.

"Rock," I sighed as I put down my music bag, "You're not going to believe it. I'll tell you in a minute, but first, can you pull up the church directory on that thing?" As he did, I grabbed the phone.

It was Gina's mother who answered, "Hi, Donna?" I could hear her daughter crying in the distant background, "It's Stacey, from church." I felt protective of them and heard it in my own voice. "I know you're concerned for your daughter. Look, Donna – tell Gina to go to the hospital if she needs to. She'll never regret taking care of herself. Tell her to listen to her body and to follow her heart. It doesn't matter if anyone thinks she's being silly. Moms have that sense of intuition. You tell her I'm for her and that I'm praying for her, okay? Let me know what you find out. Yes. I'll be praying." Donna exhaled with some relief at being acknowledged. She thanked me and hung up the phone.

Rock was staring at me, wanting to know what the heck had happened. When I finished telling him, all he could do was shake his head. We didn't like where this was heading, and we were less than six months into our two-year commitment. God help us.

It was almost all I could think about when I lay in bed awake that night, holding Gina in my prayerful thoughts.

The next morning, I was distracted, doing a puzzle with the boys on the floor, my brain still fuzzy from a night filled with replays of the service in between a few hours of short sleep. Rock was in his robe, busy cleaning up from breakfast, with a dish towel hanging over his shoulder.

The phone startled me when it rang right nearby. As I answered, I put a 'shush' finger up to my mouth, and the boys copy-catted me, making me smile.

"Hello?"

"Stacey, it's Reverend Kathryn." I mouthed her name to Rock and pointed to the phone so that he could take over with the kids while I left the room. "Hi Kathryn." I heard her exasperation when she repeated herself, "Yes, it's *Reverend* Kathryn…"

I rolled my eyes.

Oookay, well, I'm not feeling in that 'calling-you-Reverend' mood.

Her voice instantly took on a mournful tone, "You've probably heard by now that our dear little Gina lost the baby last night..." My heart sank at the news. Kathryn continued, "... as I had suspected." *Umm... excuse me? Are you actually going to lie straight to me right now, as if you hadn't completely discounted her last night.*

I couldn't believe that she would have the audacity to pretend like I hadn't heard what she had actually said. I had to calm my breathing quickly to hear the rest, "I'm going to ask that you not contact Gina until I talk to her. She'll be very upset, I know, and I know that you want to reach out and pour all that love you have on her." Her voice was sickeningly sweet, and I knew something was up. I was getting nauseous. "But as her minister," she continued, "I need to perform rites on her and the baby.... *You* understand." I didn't even have a chance to reply before the phone clicked and hummed in my ear. As if I didn't know what she was doing, setting herself up as the caring one and me as the problem.

The honeymoon at the new church was officially over.

The Great Unraveling

"A sudden, bold, and unexpected question doth many times surprise a man and lay him open."

Francis Bacon

The stunning Fall colors inspired weekend drives into nearby Massachusetts and Vermont. The car had become a sanctuary. Even the kids were silent in some kind of sacred autumnal awe, at least until we'd happen upon a fabulous vista of trees, and then they'd break into a chorus of 'oohs' and 'ahhs.' You'd never find a California palm tree adorned with these vibrant shades of Fall. I was pretty sure God had created these here in the North East as a reward for the people brave enough to endure the long, blank and bleak winter that quickly follows, and seems to last forever.

Those sweet moments shifted into memories overnight. An icy December, full of below-freezing temps and high winds, brought that pioneer feeling to both Rock and me as we adjusted to life in the North East. Drafty houses, electricity outages, and flooded basements were common topics while standing on line at the post office. Gutters were full of wet leaves needing to be cleaned before more of the snow jammed them into the drain pipes and turned them into a moldy, congested mess. And that damn pile of wood... the one that should have been chopped a few months back still sat outside, waiting to be tended to and brought in for the fireplace. These were only a sampling of the reminders that we were still so new to this.

Living in the North East was not for the faint of heart.

Inside didn't seem much better. A collection of unopened moving boxes that still remained in the laundry room called to me along with the piles of dirty clothes. Moving to the East Coast didn't heal my laundry avoidance issues like I thought it would.

Or the peace issues either.

In fact, things seemed to be getting worse.

My head was swirling from the growing tensions with Kathryn, along with her tensions with the board. And my tight-rope walk between the two. The demands of the upcoming holidays at the church — with new liturgies for me to learn, songs to practice, and a choir to assemble — were all-consuming.

And then, there was my family that needed me too.

It was a wonder anyone actually got to think about God in the middle of trying to celebrate holidays that were supposed to be about Him.

Despite the temptation to work in my warm home on this freezing Saturday morning, Rock announced, "We're taking a family walk down to the village."

Blech.

Do I have to?

Can't you all go without me?

I was so tired, and I honestly didn't feel well.

As if reading my mind, Rock pointed at me, "And don't you get any ideas, missy… you're coming with us. It'll do you good."

The kids cheered. I inwardly groaned but flashed a weak smile to the boys. They loved me and wanted to be with me.

Why am I always so frustrated lately?

The 'rest' time with my inconsistent stillness practice might as well have been called the 'restless' time. The few times I did sit down, more stuff came bubbling up. Questions about God, *"What is the deal with all these rules? Who are we supposed to love, and who are we supposed to save? Why am I trying to win people to my theology when they seem more peaceful and free than I am? What if I just took all the things that I believed off the table and started over – would I risk everything… like my salvation? Would you punish me, God?"*

I realized that my spiritual beliefs were woven throughout every part of my life — including my job — and if I kept pulling this thread, everything would unravel.

Including me.

Who would I be without these beliefs in God?

I would get up and distract myself with busy work. No answers came quickly to the questions rattling around inside of me, leaving me on edge and feeling farther and farther away from my family and less patient with pretty much everything.

Please, God... help me. How is it that I am doing this stillness practice to gain peace and yet I'm getting just the opposite? What am I doing wrong this time?

I always felt like I was the problem.

It didn't help matters that the questions weren't staying on the inside. I didn't understand why we were performing certain rituals in the liturgy at church, and when I would present my questions to Kathryn, it just seemed to her like more insubordination.

Everything was just building up inside of me and I didn't know where to turn. I didn't want to distract my friends from my old church back in California, and I didn't want to confuse or concern the parishioners of our current church in the weekly meetings we had in our home.

Kathryn wasn't at all excited about my questions. She impatiently huffed and tugged at her collar while the red crept up the sides of her neck. And God, well... my questions were *about* God. So how do you talk to God when one part of you is wondering if you'll be punished for your doubts, and the other part of you is questioning if that god is even real to begin with?

So much. Just so, so much.

I sighed audibly, noticing the faces staring at me, excited and ready to go on our trek.

Resentfully, I started pulling out all the layers of clothing for the kids and me. I felt too guilty to say 'no' again, but it was so hard to be around them these days. Their needs and noises felt like so much, especially on top of all the noise already taking up space in my head.

We bundled everyone, locked up the house, and started our walk down to the river village.

The sky had that wintery white, low cloud cover that made it dim and yet squinty bright all at the same time. The kids didn't notice. They just happily picked up sticks and giggled, bouncing into each other's padded clothing and bounding off again down the hill. Rock put an arm around me and pulled me in.

"Come on, Sta, lighten up. This'll be fun!" My arms were tight around me. Despite the layers and his strong hug, I couldn't get that chill out of my body. "We'll hit the 'peasant store' and get the kids some of those big cookies before we head to the river."

I playfully hit him on the arm, "Stop calling them that. Be nice, Mr. Robbins." He finally got a smile out of me.

"Wha–?" Rock hugged me tighter while feigning innocence.

The 'peasant store' he was referring to was run by The New Disciples: a religious community that had no church but lived together communally. They believed that they were the only ones enlightened about Jesus, and if you were enlightened too, you'd give up all your material possessions and come live with them. The other churches in the area had warned us when we first arrived: "They're a *cult.*"

Hmmm…

Undaunted by the warnings, and curious about their beliefs, I had attended one of their 'getting-to-know-you' meetings for the local residents a few months back. It was held behind their store, which made you feel like you had just taken some kind of time-machine trip back to the late 1800s. Wood all around, pewter cups and hand torn chunks of warm bread from grain they had grown – and ground into flour – before they baked it themselves. They gave each other Hebrew names, drank Yerba Mate, and taught their kids to work hard and help each other.

I dug their kindness and that they were living a part-pilgrim/part-hippie kind of crunchy granola lifestyle. But after hearing their message (a cross between dull and militant), I decided that I would just enjoy them without having to agree with them.

After the meeting, Josiah, one of the eager new recruits, came to talk me into joining their community. I was trying to find a gracious way to decline, "Thanks, Josiah, but really...I'm good." That's when he examined my face in a confident and quizzical way, "But are you *satisfied*?" I paused and searched his face to see if I should trust him with my God-questions but decided against it. I didn't have an answer for him – or at least an answer I wanted to give – but Josiah's question had haunted me ever since.

At the end of the meeting, they handed out boring pamphlets with long sentences and teeny-tiny fonts – too small to read if you weren't interested – and the most delicious ginger cookies I'd ever had in my life.

Rock squeezed my arm and went on, "They're nice people in there... strange, but nice. And they make a mean cookie, but hey, it's not my fault they dress like the peasant extras from Star Trek."

I rolled my eyes and leaned into his hug. That's all we needed, the kids walking in there and calling them 'peasant people.'

"WEEEEEE!!!!!"

The boys gleefully ran the last bit of the way down the steep sidewalk, squealing with delight before they stopped at the front door of the store. Little bells jingling from the opening door were a welcome, festive sound, and the boys headed straight to the basket with the hand-carved wooden toys.

"Careful boys… be gentle," I said to Thing 1 and Thing 2, who weren't paying attention to me at all.

Rivkah was working the counter. She was the oldest woman in the community, in her late 60s, and their resident healer, using natural remedies and herbs.

"Hi, Rivkah. We will take a half-dozen of your unbelievably delicious ginger cookies, please."

"Hello, Stacey…Rocky." She smiled and nodded to each of us. "The batter's just being made, so they'll need to rest before they're baked. It will be about an hour."

"That's fine," I answered. "We'll go down to the river first and pick them up on the way back up the hill." I peeked around at the store's different soaps and sweaters that were all hand-made by their community members, when Rivkah handed me a hot carob drink to taste. They didn't do chocolate – reason enough for me not to join their ranks.

I nodded my thanks at her generosity and took a gentle drink of the warm concoction. It was surprisingly yummy and had a hint of an herb that soothed me as I sipped it.

I exhaled and pulled my hat off while in the warm store. She was still standing there, looking at me.

"How are you feeling, Stacey? You look a touch pale…" I heard a sincerity in her question that disarmed me enough to answer with more information than I had planned.

"You know, I've been having a hard time... getting strange fevers and chills the last month or so – they just come and go, and I can't figure out the pattern." I paused, trying to think of anything else, "Oh, and my hair's been falling out like crazy. I'm sure it's just my usual lack of sleep, on top of all the adjustment to the workload of everything: church, home life, and the transitions of the seasons... *you know*? I haven't lived on the East Coast in 20 years, and the temperatures are hitting me much differently than when I was a child." She nodded in understanding. "Is it colder than it was 20 years ago, or am I just getting old and dealing with a cranky thyroid that still needs to adjust?"

She raised her eyebrows and smiled.

"Why don't you quit your job?" Rivkah was not one to mince words. Her solution made me laugh and was very true to the culture of her community where the men went out to work while the women stayed and did the more domestic jobs. I answered, "The reason we came out here was *because* of my job."

"Yes, but why doesn't Rock just do it so that you can stay home with the boys?"

I thought, *Oh God. That's not my reality. Plus, I don't want to stay home full time with the boys.*

I feel so inept as a mom lately, even though I'm completely devoted. I have a very high standard for myself, and I'm feeling insecure about every aspect of my life – wife, mom, ministry leader. The last place I want to fail is at being a mom.

But instead, I said, "We're a team. We do our music together, our parenting together – we've just always worked together, and I love that."

And I did – but I knew there was more to my 'why' these days.

"Well, if you were here with us – in our community – Rock would work with the men while the women helped you with the children. The Holy Spirit would help us all."

I smiled at her attempt to 'win one for the team.' The thought of being away from the church complications with Kathryn and having more help with the boys was tempting, but the price tag of having to adopt their theology just wasn't worth it. I shook my head, "Thank you for the offer, but I'm sure that I'll find my balance. It just takes time, right?"

She shook her head and stated evenly, "No. It takes the Holy Spirit to have balance, and you don't have the Holy Spirit."

My insides got whiplash.

What did she just say...

Out loud?

Straight to my face?

I turned, shocked, scanning her eyes to see if she was kidding. She wasn't. In fact, she didn't even blink. She just smiled and stared back as if she'd just told me it was going to be 70 degrees and sunny tomorrow. I'm not sure why, but for some strange reason, after the initial shock, it struck me as sassy-old-lady *amusing* instead of completely-uncalled-for *rude*.

It's the Holy Spirit that's keeping me from punching your lights out right now – is what my inner smart aleck was thinking.

I had been taught that the Holy Spirit was with me ever since I said "Yes!" to Jees-us! What was she talking about?

I didn't want to get into it, and didn't know what to say. I was still kind of in shock, so I just let it drop and turned to see if my husband had caught any of this. If he had, he was probably getting brain damage from rolling his eyes.

But Rock had missed the whole exchange while trying on some work boots. He was shaking his head in that 'No thanks' way to the earthy looking young man with a long ponytail who was helping. I could tell from my husband's face that his 'peasant dance card' was full. His voice carried through the little store, "Come on, gang – let's get going. There are some river rocks with our names on them!"

Caleb came up to me, tugging my jacket, "Cookies, Momma?" Seth was right behind him, nodding enthusiastically.

"They're still in the oven, but they'll be ready after our fun at the river, okay?" I turned to Rivkah, "We'll pick them up on our way back home. You'll set them aside for us?"

She affirmed, "Of course, of course." She nodded to the boys with her grandmotherly assurance, and they thanked her with happy grins and cheers in their outside voices even though they were standing right next to me.

Between the loud children and the spiritual insinuations, I needed to get some air.

Do I have the Holy Spirit, God? I always read about that one sin – that infamously vague, 'unpardonable' sin that could make the Holy Spirit leave me. Did I do that, God, in all this screwing up of my life and faith? Did I make you leave and never want to return?

Is that why I don't have peace like I want – and like I should?

Could Rivkah be right?

The questions were like arrows assaulting my mind before they ricocheted down to stab my heart.

Ugggh…I bent over in a groan on the river dock. The feeling was too much, and cramps came strong in my stomach. The physical pain distracted me from the emotional. Maybe the carob drink was hitting me wrong.

I waited a minute. But when I straightened up, a woozy feeling came over me. I grabbed the rail to my right and caught a view of the boys and Rock on the river's edge throwing stones, lost in complete happiness.

They don't need me. I'm just getting in the way of the wonderful life they could have. They'd be better off without me.

The thought brought tears to my eyes. I shook my head to make it all stop. I knew it was a lie, but there was also a part that sounded so… so *reasonable*.

They're right here and I'm missing them…

A profound sadness washed over me as I made my way off the swaying dock back to the boys. Walking slowly gave me some time to recenter while the worst of the painful feelings in my body and heart subsided.

Rock put his hand up like a stop sign: "You guys stay here. I don't want to be in the store forever. We have to get back home." He ran in to get the cookies while I stayed in the fresh air with the boys. It was fine he was going in alone, I didn't really need another run-in with Sister Mary Sunshine.

"Look, Momma!" Caleb held his cookie up in front of his face. The treat completely covered it, and he was so proud. He must have remembered me saying at some point that they were bigger than their heads, so Seth started doing it too. It was good to laugh and be distracted for the moment while our happy little customers chatted, chomped, and stomped their way up the hill.

Caleb turned around, walking backwards up the steep climb to face me, "Momma, can we have a dance party when we get home? All together?" He seemed so big at three and a half. *My little man...* "Yes," I promised, "We'll do one. All together."

Ugh.

Not my favorite thing. The dance party consisted of running in circles around a support pole in the low-ceiling basement while crazy 'kid' music blared from the speakers. I was already looking for an excuse. He said with his little lisp, "Come on Seff – Momma's gonna do it, too! Let's run!" And they took off the best that two little squirts in snowsuits possibly could – leaving a trail of cookie crumbs behind.

Breathless and pink-cheeked, they arrived at the front door a few steps before us and were ringing the doorbell a thousand times.

"All right, all right... enough already." Rock reached over their tiny heads to get the key into the lock.

In between the "ding dongs" of the bell, I could hear that the phone was ringing. I felt like we were on a TV game show: one of us had to hurry to get the door open; the other had to jump the kid-hurdle; and someone had to answer the phone.

"Hello? Hello?" I said in a breathless rush.

"Stacey?" The connection sounded sketchy. "Stace, can you hear me? It's Nancy... from Alaska. We had a phone appointment today, honey."

Shoot!

I completely spaced out. LIfe just kept falling through the cracks. I couldn't tell if it was too much life or too many cracks.

"Oh, Nance – I'm sorry, hold on a minute..."

"Rock?" I covered the phone and whispered to him, "Can you take the kids downstairs and start the dance party while I talk to Nancy?" I pleaded with my eyes.

He gave me that, *You told them you'd be there* kind of look. *Ugh. I know!* My eyes said back. I already felt the guilt like a knife in my heart before he twisted it another turn.

"You guys start. I'll join you soon..." I made another promise that I knew I would break. He closed the basement door behind him and padded down the stairs with his stocking feet and two little boys while I got situated on the couch.

"Nance, how you doing?"

"Good. Good, Stace! Honey, the question is, how are *you*?"

The pause on my end was significant. I didn't know where to start.

She jumped back in, "Actually, Stace – listen, the most important question on my heart for you right now is this:

Are you resting?"

Before I could say anything, as if on cue, the disco version of 'The Hamster Dance' started thumping through the floors from the basement below.

I sighed.

Resting... hmmm... let's see. You want the short answer

Or the long one?

12

The God of 'No'

"To be great is to be misunderstood."
Ralph Waldo Emerson

The short answer:

Kinda.

Not really…

Actually, no.

The longer answer:

I had started to, but it was freaking me out.

Nancy was listening, so I just blabbered away,

"Ahhh… Nance… It's just so hard. I don't know if you'll understand because you live in freakin' Alaska with like nothing around you and haven't just moved 3,000 miles with two young kids…"

I heard the 'story' in my voice. There was a part of me that had turned my life into a mantra of excuses, repeating the same thing I had said eight months ago when we arrived.

But it didn't stop me.

"It's just there's so much to do. Everyday, it's on my list – honestly! I mean, it's the list that I can't find because I don't know where I put it. For some reason, I can't find a rhythm to my day either, so it never seems like there's a consistent time. That's my story at home, but then, there's work. I can't schedule the fires that need to be put out at church with all the responsibilities there."

I took just enough breath to keep the narrative going.

"And I just haven't been feeling well. So, the times when I *do* have good energy and feel okay, I spend racing around trying to catch up on all the places I'm behind. So, I've done it a few times here and there, but taking time to rest feels so… self-indulgent… and so wasteful."

I was blathering so many justifications. I wasn't even sure I was making any sense.

I waited for her to jump in and protest but she just said, "Is there more?"

I told her about the guilt of feeling like I was missing my kids growing up and about living with a husband I had practically turned into a nanny as I was dealing with all the work stuff.

I told her about how Kathryn seemed to have crawled up my butt and into my head at the same time and taken residence in both places. That I spent night after night awake with insomnia, trying to figure out how to say things just the right way that would cause the least amount of damage. Since winning was no longer an option, my life at the church became about trying to lose less.

The perfect example came flying out of my mouth with the next breath… about how the bishop had arrived and asked Kathryn how our attendance was on one particular holy day.

"Oh! We were quite thrilled to have over 100 in attendance!" she declared proudly.

He nodded approvingly, pleased to know that a church that usually hosted 15-25 people on a Sunday would have that much growth. She was beaming – until I opened my big mouth. I glanced down at my notes, distracted by the numbers being thrown around. "I'm sorry... I see that we had 29. Remember, Kathryn?" I innocently asked, taking a second look at my notes to confirm. "That was the day of the Martin's son's christening, and so we had extra guests." I didn't even have to look – I just felt Kathryn's body tighten as she turned away from me. The tension was palpable as the board glanced nervously around. Mercifully, someone brought up the next item on the agenda, and we moved on.

Oh crap.

I shot a glance to my friend, Molly, sitting across from Kathryn and me.

Molly was a dry-witted, straight-shooting, loyal woman with straight hair that wouldn't do anything but sit in a sensible bob on her shoulders. Her deadpan delivery of life in the church kept me in stitches, and she had become one of my only true friends from the congregation. She was one of the brave ones who came to me asking, "What the hell is up with Kathryn and you?" when everyone else was cowering in the face of Reverend Kathryn's religious peer pressure. I understood. In a small town, there is no place to run and hide. And in a small church, there is no back pew to get lost in. If you say something, you have to face it. And here in this small church, Kathryn was not only a formidable and intimidating opponent, she was their God representative.

People were afraid of her.

Molly was one of those admirable people who seemed to live within the community but outside the pressures of it. She called things as she saw them, and people respected her for it. This also earned her a trusted seat on the board.

The moment that I said what I did, in front of the bishop, I saw her lift her hand up to her forehead, covering her eyes, and thereby avoiding Kathryn's intense reaction. It was official – I had screwed up – again. I was just in 'being accurate' mode, thinking I was being helpful because I had actually stood in the back of the church and counted that day – like she told me to do each week so that we could have an accurate headcount. I was just doing my job. I wasn't even thinking that I had just made her look like a liar in front of her boss.

Or me, like a Judas in front of mine.

I approached my boss the next day. She was stiff and guarded, her collar on tightly and her eyebrows slightly raised.

"Kathryn, I am so sorry. I didn't mean to…"

I didn't know what to say…

Disagree with you?

Embarrass you?

Correct you?

"I mean, Nance, why wasn't she apologizing to me for lying and putting all of us who knew better, in that awkward situation?"

Nancy just sighed with a "hmmm…"

While I was trying to think of the best way to finish my apology, Kathryn turned and left, behind the usual cloud of disappointment.

That's why I kept it to myself when Gertrude ("that contentious, old woman," as Kathryn called her — the lone, faithful office staff for the last 30 years) was muttering loudly one day when I walked into the church office. She was sitting alone at the desk pouring over two white books in front of her.

Her gray-and-white hair was cut short and permed into submission against her head. She wore no make-up, except for bright coral lipstick. She was an enigma in orthopedic sneakers, jeans, and an open sweater that hit right at the unflattering vicinity of the hips, but when she swiveled around, her t-shirt was full of kids' smudge-y handprints and paintings of stones with the big, messy letters, "Grandma ROCKS!" on it.

"What's up, Gertie?"

I made the mistake of asking.

She would have told anyone willing to listen, but it just happened to be me. "I knew that woman was up to something, Stacey! If someone visits once – comes to a wedding or baptism and signs our guest book – Kathryn turns them into a permanent member of our parish." Sure enough, when I checked the member book, Gertie was right. It looked like the numbers were increasing at a pretty good pace since Kathryn had arrived, yet the size of our congregation wasn't significantly changing each week.

"Yes, Stacey, but that's not the bigger problem. We send tithes to the bishop based on how many people we have in our church, and in order for her to keep up this charade, she's been draining our accounts in order to gain favor with the bishop and make it appear like we have more people than we actually do!"

I wished that I could have turned back the clock and never asked Gertie what was up.

It was too much to know, but she had more...

After the last public faux pas with the bishop, Kathryn had taken him out to lunch and, apparently, raked me over the coals. I became *persona non grata* at any future occasions when he was in town.

In fact, the next time he was scheduled to arrive, Kathryn came to me, "I have a very, very important job for you during the meeting, Stacey..." Her seriousness left me quiet as I nodded and followed her around the corner. She led me out of the church and into the parking lot that had a section cordoned off by the office. Kathryn handed me a box of chalk and a map.

My job was to watch the children.

And take them throughout the village on a scavenger hunt.

It wasn't enough that I not attend the meeting; she didn't even want me on the campus. I wasn't even sure it was legal to take the kids on a parade through town, but Kathryn was very clear that I was to take them away from the church for the hour-long meeting after service.

The 'rewards' for being honest...

Not.

This was a familiar feeling.

I remember getting a little laminated card from a friend to put in my purse after I said "Yes" to Jee-sus.

It had a pretty rainbow on it, with an Unknown author and it was entitled, "God Said, No."

I asked God to grant me patience.
God said, "No."
"Patience is a byproduct of tribulations; it isn't granted, it is earned."
I asked God to give me happiness.
God said, "No."
"I give you blessings. Happiness is up to you."
I asked God to spare me pain.
God said, "No."
"Suffering draws you apart from worldly cares and brings you closer to me."
I asked God to make my spirit grow.
God said, "No."
"You must grow on your own, but I will prune you to make you fruitful."
I asked God for all things that I might enjoy in life.
God said, "No."
"I will give you life so that you may enjoy all things."
I asked God to help me LOVE others, as much as God loves me.
God said, "...Ahhh, finally you have the idea."

As a kid who was into music, lyrics, and prose, I loved all of this because it was poetic. I didn't realize that the God of that poem comprised a theology that was at the heart of my restlessness — quite literally, the reason for my lack of 'rest.'

The theology that says the best part about being a Christian is suffering and being happy about it.

And theology that says, this is God's specialty: Trading my prayer requests for suffering.

So, I learned over the years to couch my true desires into noble prayers instead of honest ones because I didn't want God to torture me if I asked for patience or blessings.

As if being dishonest with yourself and with God isn't enough of a slow, guilty torture...

"Go on..." Nancy was patiently listening. I didn't know how to tell her the next part. The real part. Which was the scariest part of it all.

I didn't want to tell her that when I sat long enough to silence the to-do list, something else kept happening, feelings of wild mistrust in God that I didn't know how to reconcile would almost instantly overwhelm me. They bombarded my heart whenever I took a moment to be quiet. There was no comfort, no relief. I was sitting with someone I didn't trust in order to learn how to trust Him. You'd have to be crazy to do that. And that's how I felt every time I tried to rest – 'crazy.' The theologies of a God who punished on a whim, without rhyme or reason, as far as I could see, would surface. Which would make me wonder: *Why would I sit with a God who was so quick to punish me for the littlest thing I did wrong? A God who would give me the opposite of what I asked for – or give it to me in a way that was so very painful?*

Just like on that stupid card I had as a kid. I show up asking for rest, and God says, "No."

Yet, it wasn't all that or only that. There was still a part of me that held onto the idea that God was 'good.' On one hand, I believed that to be true, but on the other, I wondered, *Is He only good as long as I'm good? As long as I've kept my end of the 'being good' deal? Then, he would protect me and bless me and save me – but if I didn't, then he wouldn't – all deals were off?*

The list Carol had given me all those years ago — how to pray and live and do everything — had become like the fine print on a legal document I had signed with God to keep my end of the bargain so that He wouldn't send me to Hell. It seemed like I didn't just have to be good. It seemed like I had to be perfect.

And any possibility of that was ruined a long, long time ago.

———————————

After the rape and my 'finding Jesus' time, I lived a very clean life…for a while.

But then, I ruined that too. As a teen, I drifted into dating, which led to things that I'm pretty sure weren't on the 'good girl' list.

Plus, I still hadn't told my parents what had happened to me. I was living that lie daily until I was 18. I finally broke down during a fight my dad and I were having over a phone bill to a long-distance boyfriend.

"You don't even KNOW me! You don't know ANYTHING about me! You don't even know that I was raped five years ago!"

I finally blurted out what had been living on the surface of my heart and mind.

Every day.

Since I was 12.

And I broke their hearts.

The shock of pain on their faces was unbearable to see. I buried my face in my pillow. When my sobbing stopped, I lifted my head to see why it was so quiet. Peeling the strands of tear-drenched hair off of my face and opening my eyes, I looked up to face their pain – but they were gone.

In the face of my honesty, they left.

No one held me.

No one comforted me.

Later, I heard my mother pacing in the hallway, angrily exhaling the smoke from her cigarette and demanding, "WHO did this to you? WHO did this?" She'd open my door and scream it again, "TELL ME! WHO DID THIS TO YOU?"

My father came in with a look I'd never seen and that I could only describe as fierce pain, anger, and confusion mixed together. He sank his imposing body down hard on the side of my bed and grabbed me so hard I thought he might hit me as he had in times before. But instead, he buried his head into my arms and just kept saying, "I'm so sorry. I'm so sorry..."

Oh God...

What had I done?

He pulled back so that I could see his face, streaked with angry tears. He grabbed my arms hard and stared into my eyes in that indescribable way that happens when pain and love collide. He shook me, "Tell me his name, Stacey! Tell me who it was!"

I know that he loved me. They both did.

But I shook my head. They had been too unreliable dealing with their own emotions with each other and with us kids. I didn't trust them.

I didn't trust that my father wouldn't kill the guy, and I didn't trust that my mother wouldn't kill herself. I didn't want to visit one parent in a jail and the other at a gravesite.

When people don't prove their stability during the regular circumstances of life, it's scary to think what they'll do during the extreme ones.

I just

Couldn't

Trust.

Not them –

And not the God who seemed to be like them.

I told Nancy some of this, and some of it she already knew from our year of talking together before our move to New York. But I was too scared to tell her the whole truth – that I did not trust God.

Part of it was that my journey seemed so different from hers. I was afraid of freaking her out with my honesty. I was afraid she'd feel like she had to save me from spiritually falling off a cliff or maybe even jumping off one.

But mostly, I wasn't even sure how deep the mistrust went. I was too scared to know.

I hinted at it in safe ways to Nancy, "I'm just struggling, Nance – on every level – relationally, physically, spiritually…" but I was afraid to utter the most salient words out loud.

Could I really tell this God how deeply I didn't trust Him?

Would He punish me for being that honest?

I was afraid to tell her that I felt like I needed to be in the witness protection program from God. But, of course, that wasn't possible since God was everywhere. There was no place to hide. I couldn't hide my questions. I couldn't hide from God's answers. I felt vulnerable all the time, and trying to 'rest' in this stillness practice was making it worse.

I was so confused… so *conflicted.*

So, I kept those scary parts to myself.

I had a desire for peace. I had a 'rest' message that was stalking me and a 'be still' thing that just seemed elusive. I had an inner-knowing that it was all connected, but hell if I knew how.

Nancy was quiet. She took a deep breath. I knew what was coming.

"Stace, do you think you were supposed to go to New York?"

"100% Nance – it was crystal clear to me."

"And do you believe that God gave you a message to rest?"

"100% again — Broadway lights kinda 'holy-freakin'-crow' sort of message."

The phone went quiet for a moment.

"Then, don't you think that the God who gave you the message and brought you there knows how to help you to rest while you're in New York?"

It was my turn to be quiet and take a deep breath.

Because that's what you do when someone asks you a rhetorical question — and also makes a very good point.

Stirring the Pot

"And you? When will you begin that long journey into yourself?"

Rumi

My husband was sitting on the couch reading with the boys when I stomped in, "Rock, I'm setting the timer for 15 minutes." I pointed to the oven timer and then to him, "If you see me before then, shoot me."

He raised his eyebrows, "Sounds a bit extreme, don't you think?"

"Yeah, well, I'm not kidding." I pushed the buttons until it got to 15 minutes, spun around and marched down the hall into my bedroom and slammed the door. I heard Caleb ask, "Daddy? What did Momma do? Is she in time-out?"

Yeah. It felt like it. But I was determined. OK, more like desperate. And besides, Nancy had spanked me.

"Stacey, I'm going to take off the gloves because I love you, so listen up, and listen up *good:* God gave you a HUGE gift in Harrisburg... yes, BUT He gave you a HUGE message too. And honey, you're not doing a damn thing about it."

Wow.

Nancy swears.

Cool.

"Do you know how many people are praying for answers HALF as clear as the one you got?"

A childhood flashback of me, being miserable sitting at our dinner table came to mind. I was seven and didn't want to eat the cold piece of meat that was grossing me out. I could see the veins and muscle and that little piece of wiggly fat that made my throat close the minute I put it near my lips. While tears streamed, I was regaled with stories about the infamous 'starving children in Ethiopia.' And 'don't you know how grateful they would be to have that piece of steak??' All I could think was: *send it to them.* But my parents would not have been amused. And neither would Nancy if I suggested sending the resounding 'rest' message that was bombarding *me*, on to those *other people* begging for their own clear signs from God.

So, I stayed quiet. And she kept going.

"So, you're just going to have to sit yourself down and do whatever it takes to make it happen. No more excuses. You're resting. That's it. Done."

Nancy had never been tough on me.

And that's why I was now lying in bed, tapping my fingers.

Because of Nancy.

It was all her fault.

I spent the better part of my resting time blaming her for the laundry not getting done and the dishwasher not being emptied. Somewhere in the middle of my rant, the timer finally went off.

Day one down.

A million freakin' days to go...

Sigh.

I prayed mostly one steady prayer that first month. Between whining and rolling my eyeballs, it went something like this:

"God, please make this time pass quickly."

Very inspiring.

Very mature.

My three-year-old had more self-control.

After that first ridiculously endless month of daily sessions — each feeling like the longest 15 minutes of my life — I perched myself on the bed, prepared for yet another utterly unproductive, useless time of counting bumps on the ceiling and searching for unicorns. But a few minutes before the blessed end, I found myself silently sinking down and relaxing. A dream-like haze took over, and I found myself in a trance somewhere between wakefulness and sleep.

Beep. Beep. Beep.

Oh my gosh. If the timer woke me up, that must have meant I was asleep – or something close to it! I ran out of the room and found The Man in the kitchen. I forgot I had my socks on and almost slid right into him. He grabbed my arm to balance me.

"Whoa! Okay, sorry... I'm okay." I steadied my footing and started rambling, "Anyway, Rock I can't explain it. I went into this sleep state, well, not really sleep but kinda sleep... anyway, there was something very relaxing about it."

I could see him resisting rolling his eyes and filtering out a wide selection of snarky responses. He settled on "Uh, yeah... that's kinda what happens when you lie down."

(Right, for people like him who fall asleep on command.)

He hugged me, "I'm proud of you, hon." He meant it.

Ugh. I felt instantly foolish. *Oh my Lord, how sad is it that my husband is proud of me for something as silly and simple as this?"*

There is seriously something wrong with me.

March in the North East can make you forget that summer exists at all. We were still salting the steps, shoveling the snow, dressing and undressing the kids in and out of layers of winter togs that ended up sopping wet on the kitchen floor. It was the endless frost, as if some Winter Witch with chronic PMS cast a spell so that we'd never see the ground or feel the warm air again.

Winter wears on people. And the people in our little church were already pretty worn with so many rules and spiritual micromanagement.

Kathryn's questions were as relentless as the season we were in:

"Well, are you *praying*?"

"*How* are you praying?

"*How often* are you praying?"

"Are you reading your Bible?"

"What *part* of the Bible?"

"Are you praying the *scriptures*? Because God will honor HIs words being spoken back to Him more than *your* words."

"Are you asking for forgiveness of sins *first*? Because God won't hear our requests unless first we repent."

"Is anyone sick in your family? Are you struggling with your finances? Are you dealing with depression? Well, it's likely because you have unconfessed sin in your life or a secret you are trying to hide from God."

And on and on...

It felt like we were constantly turning over rocks to look for demons or casting out demons in all of our spare spiritual time.

To people she didn't prefer, she would say things like:

"If your life is going too easy right now, it's because you're doing the Devil's work."

Or

"If your life is too hard right now, it's because there's sin in your life."

But if she liked you, she would take the same statements and twist them:

"If your life is easy right now it's because God is blessing you for being such a wonderful soul!"

Or

"If your life is hard right now, buck up! That means you're doing something meaningful for God, and the Devil is furious and trying to distract you."

Which God was it?

I started to wonder if maybe God and Kathryn were in cahoots to make life as spiritually miserable as possible. She had all these questions, but I had my own that were surfacing during the second month of consistent 15-minute resting times.

Do you really want me to read the Bible?

Does that really make you happy – or happier with me?

Do you really want me to go to church?

Or is that something people made up to hang out with each other – or maybe to control each other but put the 'God stamp' on it to give it more authority?

Do you really want me to pray a certain way...

Or in a certain order...

For a certain length of time?

If I don't do it all the right way, will you still hear me?

Is it true that if I don't say, 'I'm sorry' to you, first, that your ears are blocked from even hearing any of my prayers? Can I really do something that would keep you from hearing me? If my heart's in the right place – or even in the wrong place – but my words are out of order, you won't help me? Really?

The questions kept coming. Kathryn, inspiring many of them. The oppressive volume of rules she demanded turned into conversations between God and me.

But it wasn't just about her. Other questions stirred that were connected to rules from my past or to my role as a worship leader, telling people to lift their hands and their hearts to the Lord so that God would come down with HIs presence.

What does that even mean? Aren't you already here — in me? In us? I asked God.

We say all these things – these words like *'blessed'* and *'grace'*... *'mercy'* and *'sin'*... we bow our heads or stand, sit, or kneel. *What is it all for if we're worshiping such a difficult-to-access God?*

After a while, I became braver with my questioning.

Do you really need all that praise and worship music? Does that do something for you?

Do you really only show up when we've sung enough songs to you? Is there a magic number of songs that unhinges something that was keeping you up in Heaven and releases you to come down – because that seems strange and makes you seem like a Jack-in-the-Box.

Are goosebumps really the sign that you've shown up? I've heard people say for years that's how they know the Holy Spirit is there – because of their goosebumps. Or is it just a sign that the musicians are good or the song moved the congregation?

Are we confusing great music with YOU?

I mean, not that you and great music don't go together, but how come I felt more spiritual listening to "Tom Sawyer" by Rush or Karen Carpenter croon some ballad when I was 13 years-old than I do when I'm singing worship songs these days?

And deeper questions still:

What about Heaven?

And what about Hell?

Why does it feel like I have to do spiritual gymnastics to reconcile that you're a god who loves us so much BUT that if we don't believe in you the right way, you'll send us to eternal punishment?

That doesn't add up.

It's like saying 2+2 = 5.

It's bad spiritual math.

How can You tell us to forgive each other, and that Jesus forgave the people who put him on the cross, but you won't forgive people for not believing in You?

Or are You saying that You do forgive us but You send us to Hell anyway? That doesn't sound like forgiveness to me.

So we're supposed to love our enemies, but if we're Your enemy, you won't love us? Isn't that hypocritical?

I'd ask the questions and then wince, waiting for the lightning bolts to strike.

I heard my inner voice saying, *"I trust Him; I trust Him not because He loves me; He loves me not."*

I was on shaky ground with all these questions. I had always been taught that questions equal insubordination.

And to make matters really scary, God, as I understood Him, just may choose to punish insubordination with death, spiritual and/or physical! I'd read the Old Testament. I knew. You might not even know you've crossed the line until it was too late.

But despite it all – and because of it all – I kept resting and I kept asking. I wasn't dead yet, so I kept on going.

I was also keenly aware that nothing was coming back to me.

Not one answer.

Nothing.

No answers. And no peace.

I was left hanging by my last jangled nerve.

———————

Caleb was sitting near me with my old Bible, vigorously flipping through the fragile, see-through pages, licking a finger on his left hand and turning pages with his right, while Seth was tripping over the toys in the living room. I was trying to plan the music for the church service that coming weekend but the sound of Caleb flipping pages was like a dripping faucet, and my stomach was doing somersaults from all of Seth's near-misses with the edge of the coffee table.

I rolled my eyeballs until my gaze landed on the ceiling.

Really, God? Really? I mean, can You get anything done with these boys around? I'm going to need a Valium to even get started.

The songs in my music folder fell on a range of anywhere between dull and insincere. None of them inspired me. How was I going to sing songs about the Trinity when I just spent the last week asking God if the Trinity was even in the Bible and why we use terms that may not even apply?

"I'm sorry, God..." I started to apologize. *Why was I apologizing?*

This was a theme surfacing during my daily resting times — the default starting point with God was, "I know I'm wrong..."

I lived in a chronic state of apologizing.

Was I repenting because I was sorry that I hurt God?

Is God even hurt-able?

Or was I repenting to avoid Hell?

If Hell was even real anyway...

Oh my Lord... here I am again, going down that same road with Him.

Crap... is God even a Him? Or is God a Her – or both – or an 'It'?

How am I going to lead the music this Sunday when half the songs espouse theologies I'm not even sure I believe in anymore?

It would be fine to have all these questions if my career consisted of polishing toenails or making flower arrangements or sandwiches for a living. It would be perfectly acceptable if I spent my business hours trading stocks or running a grocery store. I can still polish toenails if I'm not sure I believe in God the same way. I can still make a sandwich if I'm not sure what to think about Jesus. But I can't sing songs to God and pray prayers to Jesus if I'm not sure what I believe about them both. My job *was* God.

I couldn't go to my God-job and not think about my spiritual questions while I was required to perform and work at a church...

With Kathryn.

She didn't bring me out here to challenge everything she stood for, and I didn't come out here to throw out everything I believed. But that's what was happening, whether I wanted it to or not. As I took on this resting practice, my faith in everything that had brought me out here was slowly and dramatically unraveling.

The 'rest' was bringing up more questions than answers, and I felt like there was no one who could help me because no one I knew was asking the questions I was asking. The people in my life all seemed fine with God. Plus, I was in leadership, and I didn't want to take a chance on throwing folks into a tailspin while I was going through my own spiritual tornado.

I sat there, shaking my head and processing all of this, when Caleb, as if reading my thoughts, looked up from the Bible, stared straight into my eyes and said,

"Just believe, Momma."

He paused to exhale and said again,

"Just believe."

I stared back, speechless, into the sea-blue eyes of my 4-year-old. He gazed at me, and I felt so known by him. I closed my eyes and exhaled too.

Oh, I want to do just that, Caleb…I want so badly to believe.

I just don't know what to believe anymore.

That was the problem.

14

The Rabbit Hole

"Well, after this I should think nothing of falling down stairs."

Alice in Wonderland

"Kathryn, your home is just beautiful."

I sincerely meant it. I walked into the newly refurbished parsonage and immediately appreciated the distinct lack of Legos on the floor and peanut butter fingerprints on the light switches. She'd had a designer come to help her, but I knew she had done the bulk of the design herself — pristine dark wood floors; sculpted, red velvet couch; and a black marble table with a bouquet of off-white flowers in the center, while the cabinets had little peek-a-boo windows so I could see her exquisite taste in tableware.

Good Lord, you'd never want any kind of windows in my cabinets unless mismatched plastic sippy cups was your preferred design style.

Kathryn was the epitome of creativity, with her gardens out back and inspiring decor all around the house. It amazed me that someone with such an eye for beauty could be so ugly sometimes. She was like Martha Stewart on the outside and Freddy Krueger on the inside.

I sat on the red couch and immediately regretted it. The thing was apparently made for small dolls or teeny people from the Victorian era with unrealistic posture, like Kathryn and her husband, Roger. The more I tried to make myself comfortable, the more awkward I became. It reminded me of trying to sit in a preschooler's chair. Suddenly you feel all hips and butt and your legs are a thousand miles long.

I felt that way in Kathryn's house, like Alice in Wonderland after she ate the pebbles that made her grow. And like Alice, all I would be able to focus on was getting the hell out of there. I spied an armchair a few feet away and made the mistake of sitting in that instead. I fit into it, sort of the way a ring fits onto your finger in the store; you can get it over the knuckle to try on, but then, you can't quite get it off. I shot up a quick prayer: *Please God, let me be able to get out of this chair without it being attached to my rear end. I don't have a shoe horn big enough to get me out of this thing.*

"Why thank you, Stacey. That's very *kind* of you." She was using *that* voice. The voice that was like the eye of a hurricane. It was a false, untrustworthy, calm that only makes you more uneasy because you know it's heralding in the second half of the storm that could kill you. I had heard her use that voice over and over again before unleashing on some unsuspecting parishioner.

Dear God, what am I in for today?

I could not get comfortable in her house or around her. I was as ill-at-ease in the chair as I was in her presence, deeply aware of my flaws and the largeness of my imperfections in light of all of Kathryn's religious propriety. She was a small person, and she fit into her religious mindset just perfectly.

I was wearing religion the way a fat woman wears a bikini: it didn't cover my sacred parts very well and there was no place to hide all my bulges.

Kathryn situated herself. She was wearing her collar today. She usually did that when she wanted to exert authority, by showing her power as she reminded you of her position. I could feel my face flushing with fever and anticipation as she led us in afternoon prayer.

"Stacey, before we get started, there's something we need to talk about."

Here we go. My stomach was suddenly aching.

"People have been talking to me about communion."

I hated when she'd start off sentences with 'people said.' That nebulous group of invisibles she used to validate her preferences. Didn't she learn in Psych 101 that when you're confronting someone, you do it on your own behalf, and if you're going to quote someone, you have to quote someone with permission? Of course not. You can't take Psych 101 when you're busy studying *Psycho* 101.

"You've not been taking communion, and people see that as a sign of spiritual weakness..." She waved her hand in the air, searching for just the right words to cut me, "... a lack of leadership." She nodded, pleased with her choice. "They think you don't care."

Don't care?

Was she crazy? Like I was going through this hell of plumbing the spiritual depths of my soul because I didn't care?

I did my best to hold it together, but it wasn't working.

"Kathryn, I'm sure you told them it's actually the opposite." I nodded in that questioning way, seeking her assurance that we were on the same page.

She just smiled, raising one eyebrow ever so slightly. This was the sport she loved to play. I swear, the woman would have loved watching people being devoured by lions if she'd been born in a different time. I continued on in the face of her non-agreement.

"It's that I care so much about not taking the sacraments lightly that I choose not to take communion sometimes. There are times when I realize you and I are in conflict, and I choose not to take it because I know we're not at peace with each other. I wait until we talk and then, if I choose, I have communion at home with Rock."

Why was I explaining myself to someone who had already tried me, found me guilty, and was holding the rope, just waiting for the right moment to hang me. And why was I trying to defend my beliefs when I was questioning the whole thing anyway?

I felt like one of those magicians-in-training standing before a table full of place settings of fine china, wine goblets, and brass candelabras. And here I was attempting to remove the tablecloth underneath without disturbing what was on top of it. It was impossible.

I was pulling on the fabric of my relationship with God, and every tradition and theology that had been set on top of it was flying into mid-air. I had no idea what beliefs would land unbroken. I had no idea which theologies were going to survive the upheaval. But until I settled on what I firmly believed, I wanted to err on the side of more respect, not less. Kathryn knew that. She was looking to upset me, and I was giving her what she wanted. I sat forward in the chair as much as my hips would allow.

"You've told them it's because I care so much, not because I care so little, right?" I asked.

She sat back in her chair as if I had asked her if she knew the sky was blue.

"Well, of course, Stacey. But, you know... those people, they don't understand those complicated thoughts. These are simple people... and while you and I understand, they are just observing and sharing their concerns. It's my responsibility to represent them so that you can know and their voice can be heard."

I knew well enough it wasn't 'them' at all. Ever since we'd arrived, I'd witnessed Kathryn's ability for starting trouble, spreading rumors, and positioning herself in the most strategic places. I knew she wouldn't be content to have them like me if it threatened her control. Her way of gaining popularity was by creating an enemy and convincing others this enemy was a threat to them too. I was watching her systematically break down my credibility in the most seemingly-spiritual of ways. She was dismantling me. And, of course, I couldn't address it with any of them because it would play right into her portrayal of me as some renegade who was trying to overthrow her authority. I was damned if I did and damned if I didn't.

That's exactly how I had felt with God most of my life: damned if I did what He wanted, even if it wasn't my heart, and damned if I didn't obey Him and instead followed my heart. One would have me living in my own personal hell, and the other would send me straight to it.

But He *had* to be that way. He had standards. And despite His love for me, He had to keep those standards. That's what I had been taught.

That God loved me so much that He would have to send me to Hell if I didn't believe in just the right way...

Just like Kathryn had to treat me this way, this terrible, manipulative way. Because she loved God so much. She was serving Him and trying to protect the traditions of the church from the likes of me.

Was anyone else starting to see the crazy in this – or was it just me? I'd never heard anyone ask these questions. I had spent the last 30-something years in the cocoon of church, and now it was feeling like the most unsafe place I could be.

The pains in my stomach were starting again, and my body felt that feverish chill.

Was anything flying off the table of my faith going to survive?

And even more terrifying — *would I?*

———————————

Bedtime that night was full of frustrations after my visit with Kathryn. I had to take communion to maintain the respect of the congregation I was leading, but in doing so, I would be untrue to what was happening in my heart.

Why did it seem to come down to this over and over again? I couldn't reconcile it with Kathryn... and I couldn't reconcile it with God either. Everything kept coming back to that core relationship with Him.

An imagination question came to me one sleepless night. What if God and I were to climb up to the top of the Empire State Building and He asked me, "Stacey, do you love me?" My honest answer would be, "I'm just not even sure that I know what that means any more, God. But I want to know. Would You help me?"

And what if, instead of hearing my heart that truly wanted to know HIs love, He picked me up by the scrap of my neck, dangled me over the edge, and said, "Stacey, let's try this again: If you say you love Me, I'll put you back on the balcony. If you don't, then I'll drop you on your head."

Anyone with an ounce of self-preservation who knows what's good for them would say, "I LOVE YOU! I LOVE YOU!"

Why was loving this God like being in an abusive relationship?

How do I get out of this? And how do I talk to a God I don't trust about the fact that I don't trust him?

"Ugh..." I groaned in torment, tossing back and forth.

"Honey, you okay?" Rock's voice was groggy. He could usually sleep through anything. "It's like being in bed with one of the kids." He was used to me not sleeping, but tonight was worse than usual.

"Sorry. I have so much on my mind," I replied.

"Kathryn?"

"Yeah, that, and a million other things."

He patted the side of my leg and then sat up all of a sudden to touch my forehead.

"Sta, you're burning up. Do you have another fever?" Rocky asked.

I probably did, but I was so distracted. I felt lousy all the time. The hair that had been coming out in bits was now falling out in clumps. I had a rash all over my stomach and my arms, but I could hide that since the cooler weather was still here. It was too much to even think about and share with Rock. He was already carrying the heavy load of both kids and dealing with a wreck of a wife who was working all the time. The house was a mess, and we still weren't moved all the way in after almost a year. That was my fault because I couldn't pull it all together and fall apart at the same time.

"Sta, we've got to figure out what's going on with you. Doesn't Julie have a doctor friend that she can reach for you?" He searched the screen on his cell phone. "It's three hours earlier back home, it's not too late to call."

He walked to the bathroom to grab the thermometer. He didn't know that I hadn't been in touch with my friends to let them know what was going on.

I felt like a failure. I had moved out here with such high hopes of a more peaceful life and making a difference in this little village, but I just couldn't seem to get out of my own way.

I had convenient excuses since the internet connection was always going out where we lived, and cell phone coverage was spotty. But the real reason was that I was embarrassed. How was I going to just dump this on my friends who had sent me out here with all their resources, confidence, and prayers so that we could make a positive spiritual difference? And now, here my faith was completely unraveling.

A couple of times, I had tried to reach out and got friends' voicemails. I hung up. What was I going to say?

"Hi, it's Stacey. Remember me? The one who led your Bible studies and women's groups? The one you gave money to so I could move 3000 miles away to help people? The one you've trusted your faith and your kids' faith to in the most sacred dark times? Yea... well, I'm a total mess. I'm losing my mind and my faith in one fell swoop. Failing in the mom and wife departments, looking like crap, feeling like crap and pretty much finding myself in a spiritual free fall. Call me after your yoga class and before your nanny leaves for the day. 'K? Bye!"

My current reality felt so freakin' unrelatable to my old life. Who would even understand?

I was feeling more and more like there was nowhere else to turn.

15

Crash and Burn

"What the caterpillar calls the end of the world, the master calls a butterfly."

Richard Bach

"You may all be seated." Kathryn waved her hand to motion everyone to sit. It was a special occasion, and some of the clergy from the area were visiting our church, so Kathryn was using her British accent on this particular day. Everyone sat while she welcomed the guests to our 25-member congregation. They nodded, and the service proceeded with a song. As Rock and I stood up to sing, I caught the sight of Kathryn's husband bowing his head to pray. Molly told me on the sly that he was assigned to do that every time I spoke or sang to make sure no evil spirit was able to sing or speak through me.

Charming.

I led the song. The visiting ministers were in obvious delight.

Quality music wasn't an established standard in most little churches in our area. In fact, before we had arrived, the former music director, who was also the organist, was deaf. Not tone-deaf. Not figuratively speaking 'deaf.' No, bless her 76-year-old heart, she had full-on hearing loss and knew sign language. I'm talking *deaf*, deaf. I remember the first

Sunday that Rock and I were visiting and Helen was sitting at the organ. She started playing. Rocky's and my eyes grew wider and wider as Helen seemed to be playing two different songs – in three different keys – all at the same time.

So having us substantially raise the bar on the quality of music in that tiny church reflected well on Kathryn's prowess in leadership. I saw her practically preening with self-pride when she observed the reaction of her religious peers. Kathryn was on a high and began to perform the recitations. Since this was a special service, there would be these short readings followed immediately by songs. I had to follow the script closely since this service order was more nuanced than usual.

As I looked down to read, I saw that another song was approaching. I stood up at the end of the reading, prepared to sing again, but it appeared that Kathyrn had missed that cue, so I sat back down.

Oh well, fine with me. One less song to sing makes my life easier, I thought. *Especially today when there are so many songs in the program.*

But Kathryn missed the next song, too.

Molly caught my eye from the side of the altar where she was sitting. She was watching her program too and noticed both misses, shrugged her shoulders and motioned for me to stay seated – which was good because I wasn't feeling well anyway.

My face was starting to flush again with fever.

At the point in the service when the next song was to be sung, Kathryn paused. I stood and started to move toward the keyboard, but she turned her head sharply at me and glared. I stopped and looked down at my program… *Nope, this is right. This is where the song goes.* I smiled reassuringly in the senior minister's direction.

But Kathryn stopped everything and put her hand out in the air.

"The Spirit of the Lord is inspiring me to pray something spontaneously right now," she said. The congregation bowed their heads obediently. I canvased the sanctuary and noticed the guest ministers were doing the same. *What is going on?*

"We have a Spirit of Confusion in our midst, a spirit who is trying to undo us," she announced. I heard some murmurs of "Yes, Lord" out in the congregation. *What is she talking about?* Kathryn turned and locked eyes with me.

"We come against that Spirit of Confusion right now in the powerful name of Jesus!"

She's talking about me? Rock was sitting right behind me, but I felt so alone.

"We need to rid our church of this confusion right now, Lord. We ask that you would do it for us." She punctuated dramatically.

Kathryn was still praying, and I could feel the buzz of agreement coming from the congregation. They didn't know she had directed the accusation at me, but I did. I just sat back down and scanned the faces, incredulously. Kathryn ended her prayer, and everyone looked up in that dazed kind of way, getting reoriented to what we were originally doing before this 'inspiration' to pray had taken over the whole service. I turned toward Molly, who had been watching the entire time. She was standing in the doorway where only I could see her, shaking her head in disgust as the scene unfolded. She was onto Kathryn. It was the only comfort I had at the moment... the only affirmation that I wasn't crazy.

At the end of the service, I made a bee-line to my friend.

"Mol, what just happened?" I pleaded.

"Stacey," her usually calm voice was amped up, "the woman is out of her *mind*. She missed all the cues. You were fine. God, she's on a mission with you. The woman is like a pit bull."

"Seriously." I said, feeling the crash of adrenaline that had held me together during the service. "I don't get it..."

"Stace," Molly eyed me suspiciously, "you don't look right. Tell you what, I'll get the boys from the babysitter downstairs and drop them back at the house after Paul and I feed them some lunch. Have Rocky take you home right now. You guys need some time alone. And for God's sake, just let him take care of you," Molly ordered.

I nodded and sighed. She was right. My skin felt stiff and scratchy with fever. It was happening again.

Rock grabbed my coat and got me to the car. A woozy feeling came over me on the short drive down the street. This wasn't good.

He opened the front door and helped me to our bedroom. "Honey, put your pajamas on." But I was so chilled that I couldn't even take off my clothes to change into something soft. I just wrapped my robe around my church clothes and climbed under the covers.

I had felt really sick before, but never like this. This was scaring me.

How much more could I take? I didn't feel that sense of release inside of me to leave, and I didn't feel like we were done at that little church. But I also didn't know if I could do it any more. I could see my own concern mirrored on Rock's face. He stuck the old glass thermometer in my mouth, thus beginning the four-minute countdown. It was probably the only time he could get me to shut up.

"Listen, Sta... this just isn't working out. I know we felt called by God to be here, and we've got all these people supporting us from back home..." He paused to help me move the pillows around. "But this is not getting better, and I'm having a hard time believing that God called us to this... this *bullshit*." He said.

Rock almost never swore, and it always surprised me when he did. He was the consummate gentleman, and I was the sailor when the inspiration or frustration struck. Never in front of the kids, but in our private conversations, I was the one who leaned toward colorful language. I managed a weak smile without letting the thermometer drop out of my mouth.

"Mmmm..." I tried to nod my head, but everything hurt and felt heavy.

"You," he pointed at me, "just be quiet. Don't talk." He glanced at the clock on the nightstand. "You have two more minutes."

I could swear there were bugs crawling on my skin. I closed my eyes and jumped when Rocky's hand touched my forehead.

"Baby, it's okay..." His voice was soothing, and it was fading into the distance as I was drifting off.

He pulled the thermometer from my mouth. "Sta! "You're 104 degrees! What the hell is going on?" I heard him leave the room and then the medicine cabinet unlatched from the bathroom next door. My tears felt warm on the side of my face.

God, I don't know what's going on either. This all feels like one chronic torment. My mind races non-stop, my body is being torn apart and torn down, and my spirit, well... I don't know anything anymore. I don't even know who I am anymore. Or who You are.

It hurt my head to cry, but I couldn't seem to stop the stream of tears. I flipped my pillow over to find the cool side, and as I turned my body into a fetal position under the covers, I pleaded:

God, would you show me who You are?

I just need to know

Who

You

Are.

It was the last conscious thought I had before sleep stole me away.

16

The Grace to Doubt

"Doubt is a difficult animal to master because it requires that we learn the difference between doubting God and doubting what we believe about God."

Rachel Held Evans

My eyes opened to find the sun warming me through the bedroom windows that I still didn't have drapes for. I squinted my eyes closed and turned away, not quite ready for all the light at once.

Flashes of images from the last few days filled my mind: Rock standing over me with concern, giving me sips of broth; Molly sitting by me with her prayer book, whispering prayers, touching my arm and making the sign of the cross on my forehead; the boys standing at the doorway to my room, moving their lips with hushed voices saying, "Hi, Momma!" and "Love you, Momma!" before being backed into the hallway as Rocky closed the door.

This time when I opened my eyes, I was mentally ready for the light. There was no clock on my bed stand and nothing to tell me the date – there was just a who-knows-how-old cup of tea, the thermometer, and my Bible.

The Bible was covered with the mauve leather that was so popular in the late 80s when I had picked it out in the bookstore as an upgrade from my youth Bible with the frosty, Covergirl lipstick still on it from my teens. My name was embossed in silver on this more mature version, and it had traveled with me all over the country. But for the last two months, I couldn't stand to even look at it. To me, it was filled with contradictions and confusions. It had stopped being a source of comfort and guidance and had become a reminder of all that I hadn't figured out yet.

It was Kathryn's weapon against me, so it hadn't been my friend.

But looking at it at this moment was different. The fight and resistance wasn't present for some reason, and a curiosity filled me as I reached for it. My arm, that had been coiled so tightly to my body, opened up with an ache as I pulled the Bible toward me. As I propped myself up to sit, my joints reminded me that I was still recovering. I leaned my head back on the pillow and sighed. *Where do you begin when you're already in the middle?* The chapters in the book of Mark that were filled with miracles passed through my mind. *A miracle would be nice right about now.*

Leaning forward, I turned the thin pages to Mark 9. It was the story of the desperate father who wanted his son to be healed from the demons that were giving him seizures and making him throw himself into the fire.

Jesus enters the village, and the people run with excitement to greet him.

No one had been able to help the man's son, not even the disciples of Jesus, so the father ran to Jesus himself and pleaded.

179

"... If you can do anything, take pity on us and help us."

Jesus answered, repeating the man's words,

"'If you can'?" said Jesus. "Everything is possible for one who believes."

Immediately the boy's father exclaimed, "I do believe; help me overcome my unbelief!"

When Jesus saw that a crowd was running to the scene, he rebuked the impure spirit. "You deaf and mute spirit," he said, "I command you, come out of him and never enter him again."

The spirit shrieked, convulsed him violently and came out. The boy looked so much like a corpse that many said, "He's dead." But Jesus took him by the hand and lifted him to his feet, and he stood up.

I paused and let the story sink in.

God, you didn't thwap him for being honest with you, for doubting you. You didn't hate him or kill him or make fun of him. You didn't kill the son to punish the father's doubt. You addressed his mistrust, and then, you healed the boy.

My mind then traveled away from the boy and Father and onto thoughts of Thomas, more infamously known as the Bible's 'Doubting Thomas', who didn't want to leave his house when his friends told him that Christ was resurrected.

Thomas had already invested his time and followed the living Christ, only to see him crucified. The grief and the doubt were too much for him, so he closed himself in and wouldn't leave. Why would he believe in the accounts of Jesus being made alive again just to encounter more disappointment on top of his deep grief?

I need proof. And I need the proof to come to me – is the essence of what Thomas told his friends. So, what did Jesus do? Jesus went to meet him. He showed him the proof of the scars and the wounds, and Thomas, who had once believed and then doubted, believed again.

Jesus didn't reject either man, the father of the boy with the seizures – or Thomas – for any of their doubts.

I had been so afraid to let God know what I really thought of Him. Not that He didn't already know. But still, to speak those words out loud… I thought for sure I would hear some form of "How dare you!" echo back at me or show up in a passive-aggressive punishment. In my formulation, telling God I wasn't sure about Him was a precursor to my child contracting cancer or our family being in a head-on collision. Something catastrophic would certainly follow if I voiced my doubts to God.

Weren't there always consequences like that with God?

Apparently not.

My body exhaled again, and my eyes were heavy. I placed the Bible back in its place on the bedside table, exhausted and surprised by how quickly that feeling had come on.

Closing my eyes to sleep, I whispered, "God, I believe in Jesus, but I don't believe. I believe in a good God, but I don't believe. I don't really know what to believe anymore. Would you help me with my unbelief?"

I settled back into sleep, drifting off to the faint sounds of little boys with grocery bags coming through the front door.

_____

"Hey, baby." Rock was smiling, brushing the hair from my forehead.

"Mmmmm…" I kept my eyes closed but reached for his hand.

"My girl." His voice always soothed me, "It's time to eat. Molly brought you some soup. You've got to eat something."

I slipped in and out of sleep for a few more minutes before I let him help me sit up. I opened my eyes expecting sunlight only to find darkness. *It's night already?* Once Rocky knew I was stable enough in my seated position, he handed me the ceramic mug. I sipped on the warm, salty broth while he filled me in on the latest news.

"Well, Stasha, you've had quite a week. We had the doctor come over on Monday to look at you. You know these little villages still have doctors who make house calls? Amazing. Anyway, he couldn't explain the fevers but told us to just let you rest as much as possible and give you liquids throughout the day. Your fever broke by Tuesday, and you've just been a sleeping fool," he said.

My mind went into question mode.

What day is today? How are the boys?

He was reading my thoughts, "It's Thursday night. I just put the kids to bed. They've been great. So much fun. So concerned about Momma."

"They scribbled pictures for you that are on the fridge, and the other day, when I was in the bathroom, they took all your spices and threw them into a big bowl to help make you better. Sta, I know those things are a small fortune to replace, but it was so funny. I was in the bathroom and I just kept hearing them sneeze over and over. Then, there would be this big clanking noise from the metal spoon hitting the metal bowl, then more sneezes. I was like, 'What the heck is going on in there?' When I got to the kitchen: Oh. My. Gosh. There was a plume of smoke from the cayenne pepper, and God only knows what else they dumped in there. They were just sitting there, happy as clams, stirring and sneezing and stirring some more. Caleb told me, 'This is to make Momma better.' So, I let them come rub the spices on your feet while you were sleeping. They love you so much."

I put the cup down on my lap, tears streaming down my cheeks.

"Oh baby, what's wrong? Don't worry. We'll clean up the place," Rock added, wiping the tears from my face. I shook my head letting him know that wasn't what I was crying about.

"Rock…"

The moonlight coming through the windows helped us to see each other's eyes. I shook my head again. I didn't know what to say. How could I let him know that for the last year I had been emotionally unavailable, missing everyday life with the boys – distracted and in performance mode.

Here they were focused on loving me and helping me, and I had spent so much time worrying about everything from taking the wallpaper off the walls to dealing with Kathryn.

Kathryn…

Crud.

It's Thursday.

I missed my weekly meeting with Kathryn.

I sighed again. The sense of responsibility distracted me from the feelings I was having about my boys. I found myself being yanked back into work-mode, trying to sit up and get my head back in the game.

"Rock, I normally meet with Kathryn on Thursday for the Sunday service, and wait… who played for the mid-week service last night? And…" His hand on my arm stopped me mid-question.

"Stacey, I talked to Kathryn on Tuesday after your fever broke. The board was meeting that night, and I told them that you needed a month to work on your health and have some time with the boys. I put in calls to a couple of church musicians up in Kingston, and they're going to cover the next four weeks while you take some time to heal."

"But the…" I began.

"I know. The money. I called Julie and a couple of our donors to see if they would help make up the difference that the church pays us. I told them what was happening. They were more than happy to help. Oh, and Julie wants you to call her as soon as you're up for it, Sta. She had no idea what you were going through." Rock said.

Oh Julie, I don't even know what I've been going through. I still don't. How could I let you know? It was a relief to hear that the details had been handled. I wasn't used to not being the one to manage them. I felt the weight of my body sink into the pillows as I took a long sip of soup. It tasted even better after the news my husband had just given me.

"How are *you*, Rock?" I realized I hadn't even asked him how he'd been handling everything. I put my hand over his.

184

"You know, I'm good – concerned about my Stasha – but really, honey, everything is going to be fine."

How could he be so even, so consistently happy? Granted, he doesn't have that same driving ambition that I do, so he isn't constantly striving to get somewhere, and we don't feel stress in the same ways. Contentment rules in him. I don't get it. I'm like a rollercoaster lately: fine one moment, bitchy the next. I'm all over the place and he's just so…well, he's just so steady. I shook my head.

"What? What's going on in that nut of yours?" He tapped his finger on my forehead. I shrugged and lowered my eyes. "Come on, talk to me. You're never this quiet," he teased. He was so playful with me.

"Rocky, I just…"

I saw his loving eyes looking back at me. *Where do I start?*

"I don't know. There's something new going on in my conversation with God. I told Him today that I didn't believe in Him, but I mean I do, but well… I don't. I just don't think I trust Him. Partly because I think the God I've been believing in hasn't been very trustworthy. But I'm just not sure if that god is the real God." I thought I sounded like a goon once I heard myself say all that. "Is any of this making any sense? I'm sorry. I must be delusional. It makes sense in my head, but then, I say it out loud and it all sounds ridiculous." I concluded.

"Sta, look. You're okay. It's just not that hard. Remember the guidance counselor you told me about when you were 16? You told me he said that people with a complicated history sometimes make things more complicated so they can find their way through in an easy way. Maybe there's something to it. You had such a hard and confusing past, for a really long time – how could that not affect how you saw God and everything else? Now, even though I don't get it, what I *do* get is that I love you and I'm right here. You're going to be fine. We're fine. The boys are fine. God knows how to get the truth to you even if you're making things complicated."

His words comforted me.

"Now, come on, let me help you to the bathroom. Dr. Richards said that I need to get you out of bed to take a few steps. I'll watch out for the Legos if you don't look at the mess, deal? I'll clean it up. Don't worry. Just hold on to me and hang in there," He said gently.

Rock stood up and held my hands as I got out of bed. I closed my eyes and leaned my head on his shoulder. It felt good to let someone else be in charge for a change.

"Momma!" Caleb and Seth greeted me in the living room with hanging-on hugs, and for the first time in a while, I didn't feel the pressure to peel them off and get to work. I led them to the couch so that I could sit while they sprawled and crawled all over me. I still felt too weak to lift them up, but I definitely wanted them near.

"Momma's gonna kiss you a million times. Ready, set, GO!" I kissed and kissed all over their faces and heads, arms and hands, as they giggled with delight.

"Our spices helped you, Momma! We made it and put it on your feet! I kissed your toe when you were sleeping," Caleb spouted with excitement. He was such a big boy, all of a sudden.

"Oh, Caleb, thank you. It *did* make me feel better," I told him.

"Me, too, Momma!" Seth's squeaky, raspy voice jumped in.

"Yes, Seth, you helped too – thank you!" He smiled and nodded his head of curls and then buried them in my neck.

"Daddy is going to make us pancakes, and then we're going to sit and read some books together. Does that sound nice?" I asked the boys.

"Yay!!" They cheered and threw their arms in the air.

Oh my God, I love these boys.

So happy and easy to please. They just wanted to have a full tummy and be near the people they loved the most.

I wish I were like that.

My past and I had made things complicated in the here and now. I worked on creating new projects and staying as busy as I could, providing well for my family – all as a way to prove my worth and distract my mind. But I was paying a cost by living in the past and the future. I was missing the people who were right in front of me. The minute I would get present, I would feel waves of guilt and the accompanying immediate knee-jerk reactions to assuage it. Being present wasn't easy because it reminded me of all I was missing – and had already missed. Getting present reminded me that I could never pay back the countless moments where the past or the future had stolen my present. Or at least that's what I thought.

So much shame.

I had felt all of this so strongly for such a long time, but something was changing. My mind was quieter since the fevers. It's like my body used the high temperatures to burn out the mental burdens I carried, as well as the vices I typically used to numb me from the weight of it all. And because of that new quietness, I felt like I could be a different kind of honest with God. I didn't feel like I had to pretend anymore now that my secret was out to my husband, to Nancy, and to myself. The ground hadn't opened up and swallowed me for telling them the truth — not only did I not trust the God I had been taught about, I didn't even know what to believe about Him anymore. Being honest left me with more mental and emotional room. I had room to explore this God without fear of punishment.

The word that kept coming to me to describe it was 'grace.' But grace took on a new meaning for me:

It meant *'space.'*

If I had the grace to doubt, it meant I really had the space to doubt.

This thought kept coming to me: that if I allowed myself to doubt, it would somehow create room for me to believe. The pressure was off to hurry and resolve the doubt or figure out what I believed in. I no longer saw it as a problem I had to fix. And that left more room for my family, who I was enjoying for the first time in such a long time. I grabbed the boys close to me and closed my eyes.

Rocky walked in, drying his hands with the dish towel, "Now, *there's* my family. Who's ready for some pancakes?"

17

The Awakening

"For things to reveal themselves to us, we need to be ready to abandon our views about them."

Thich Nhat Hanh

It was April and the end of our first year in the village. Spring was making its appearance with warmer days, crocus, and budding Cherry Blossom trees. On our family walks down to the village, I noticed that even the ugly houses were charming with the dogwoods blooming out front.

It was odd to make the left turn down the hill and see the little church on our right. I felt the pull inside of me. *I wonder what they must be thinking.*

I knew all about those venomous words couched in spiritual phrases that Kathryn would probably be saying about us – the same way she had said them to me about the rest of the church. It was that dysfunctional part of the religious culture where people can spiritualize, gossip, and slander, and then call it 'love.'

Kathryn would have seen my doubting God as a reflection on her, in the same way she saw our musical talent as a reflection on her – and the only way she knew how to handle it was to demonize me and distance her spirituality from mine.

I wish I could tell her about the God of Thomas and how that God seems more than okay with where I'm at. That maybe my doubt is actually part of my faith, and not an enemy of it. But I don't think she'd be able to hear it from me. At least not now.

The tenderness of the little hands in mine brought me back to reality as we stepped down the crooked sidewalks of the steep hill. "Look, Momma! The river!" Caleb was so excited. Seth wasn't tall enough yet to see over the rooftops, but he copied his big brother and gasped as if he could see, too.

The door to the country store opened, and the bells jingled. The familiar sound still made me smile. Rivkah was there and helping a customer when we walked in. I waved and she nodded. She and I had mended that awkward 'Holy Spirit' moment just a few days after she had said it when she showed up unexpectedly on my front step:

"Rivkah, what are you doing? It's freezing! Get in here." She was bundled in a heavy wool coat and thick scarf, but it had to be close to twenty degrees on that winter day. I peered around to see if there was a car that had dropped her off, but there was none.

She stepped in and handed me a thermal sack. She seemed smaller and older to me.

"Did you walk all the way up here?" She nodded. "No matter." She brushed the attention with a wave of her hand. Rivkah wasn't one to complain, but I could tell she was cold. I took her coat and put it by the heater and gave her a warm blanket as she sat at the table and faced me.

Before I had a chance to ask why she was here, she spoke in her usually direct way,

"Stacey, I'm sorry for saying what I said to you the other day. You came into my store with your family, and I treated you in a way that I wouldn't want to be treated. I'm sorry."

I was about to jump in but she went on with words that surprised me, "You were very gracious with me, Stacey. Thank you."

I knew she wasn't apologizing for believing what she believed, but rather for saying it to my face and for being rude. I really respected her for coming all the way to tell me. And she seemed genuinely surprised that someone without the Holy Spirit could be kind in the face of what she had done.

"It's all good, Rivkah. I have a strong jaw from chewing on my own feet plenty of times, trust me." I saw relief in her smile.

"Is this for me?" I looked down at the thermal bag and opened it. Inside was a peace offering: two hot to-go cups of carob tea and a warm loaf of banana walnut bread. We sat, ate, and had a nice chat that afternoon before I drove her back home. We kept our conversations on the things we had in common: a deep love for our families and wanting to do our best for them. From that point on, we enjoyed more relaxed conversations with each other.

I was glad to see her working the counter at the store this Spring day:

"Rivkah! How are you?"

"Good, good, Stacey. I'll be right with you." And she scurried in the back, just in time for a big CLUNK! to come from where my boys were playing with her grandsons. The boys laughed and started restacking the wood blocks that had just fallen.

"Boys, can you ask Rivkah for some ginger cookies?" I told Caleb and Seth as Rivkah came from the back kitchen. It gave them a mission that would occupy both their hands and their mouths for a few minutes while we waited. "And Rock and I will each have a cup of tea with some raw honey, please."

She nodded and patted the bench so that the boys would sit in one place with their cookies instead of walking all over the store sharing crumbs with the floor. They put the big round treats up in front of their faces and giggled while they turned them into a game of peek-a-boo. They giggled and chomped, nodding to each other in the silly way that brothers do while they're chewing big, happy bites of delicious cookies.

While the tea was brewing, Rivkah asked me how I was doing. She had heard I was ill.

"I'm doing okay... on the mend. Feeling quiet as I'm regaining my strength."

"What did you do with the little boys for nursing while you were sick?" she asked. The community was very big on nursing for a long time, following the Hebrew tradition of nursing until a child was three to four years old. They respected me because I had shared a similar value.

"You know, it just seemed like a fitting time to stop. My body needs to repair, and the boys are big and strong enough to stop." I felt that twinge of sadness even though I knew it was for the best. I met Rivkah's gaze with mine, "I really loved nursing those two little monkeys, but it was time…" She nodded with understanding.

"Nursing brings them stillness." Her words struck me as ironic, bringing back memories to that day at Julie's house.

"Rivkah, how amazing that you said that! I met a woman who told me the German word for nursing is 'stillen.'"

"That's true," she nodded, tucking a piece of cookie inside of her mouth, taking a second to thoughtfully chew and swallow, "but it's originally a Hebrew word."

Well, she would know. The New Disciples studied Hebrew as a part of their training.

"Can you tell me what you know about it?" I asked as I went to sip my tea.

"Yes, of course…well, people understand it to be the nursing process – and it is – that's part of it. When the child is needy and hungry, the mother feeds the baby, of course, but the verb tense is future perfect, if you're getting technical about it, so it's a little different…"

I waited for her answer, but the bells on the door jingled and interrupted her thoughts as the customer walked in. Rivkah waved and smiled, then turned back to me.

"Where was I? Oh yes… 'stillen.'"

She ironed the napkin in front of her with the palm of her hand as she thought.

"It's the weaning process – the point at which the child is strong and healthy enough to start living his life without the dependence on the mother's milk. It's actually a term that promises satisfaction."

We were both quiet for a moment, but my thoughts were in motion.

Stillen...

Stillness...

Satisfaction...

They were connected.

My mind started putting the pieces together.

I thought back to a year and a half before when I'd been pacing around the bedroom after Rock told me I had no peace. The "Be still and know that I am God" scripture had been churning beneath the surface ever since.

Then, I prayed for God to help me understand this 'be still' message He had been trying to send me for so long.

The German woman who had appeared out of nowhere and told me the word 'stillen.'

Months later, the stranger, Josiah, who had asked me the haunting question, "Are you satisfied?"

And now, here was Rivkah, filling in another piece to this seeming puzzle.

She stepped away to help someone, and I walked to the back room that overlooked the river to process it all.

I closed my eyes.

The Spirit had been sending me one message after another for almost two years…well, probably my whole life, but I had never really noticed..

When God said, "Be still and know that I am God…" this is now what I heard:

Stacey, be satisfied, knowing that I am who I am and you are who you are. I made you, and I have been feeding you with the truth of both of those things, getting you ready to live a strong life.

Be satisfied.

Be full with this knowing.

No more of that crazy hunger, neediness, like the baby restless for the milk it feels insecure will be there.

Be satisfied, knowing that I will always be there for you, that you can trust Me and My love for you. That you are filled with it. With Me. In you. And where you don't yet trust Me, you can rest and be satisfied in knowing that I'll get you there, because I made you, and I love you.

He chose to take me along this path of revelation by inviting me to come to Him.

And *rest.*

The words from Jesus, "Come to me, all you who are weary and burdened, and I will give you rest." had such deeper meaning now.

I had been so weary.

And needed such rest.

Who knew that resting physically was going to lead me to spiritual rest?

And that rest was about trust.

And that trust was about peace.

Peace. That's what I had longed for

For such a long time...

I wasn't there yet. Closer than I was, but still...

This changed *everything*.

18

Right Between the Eyes

"'Cause there's a lesson in here somewhere... and I know it's mine."

Jude Cole

We spent many days walking down to the river in those first few weeks. Rock would watch the boys while I sat and rested on the swaying dock. If I tried to stand, I'd spend the whole time trying to keep my balance, but as soon as I sat, the rocking that had threatened me moments before, now lulled me.

The lesson wasn't lost on me.

In those resting times, there was so much space in my mind, that whatever needed to come to the surface was able to. Images and memories would come. Some would just flash by, and some would linger as if they wanted to tell me something.

The memory of a women's retreat in California many years before kept appearing.

My new friend, Claire, was a well-known philanthropist and speaker at this event that I was attending. The word was out that Claire had taken me under her wing. The women were abuzz that I was getting this opportunity to be mentored by her, and one of the leaders at the retreat asked me to introduce Claire to the audience before she spoke. Of course, I said yes, but it wasn't a clean-in-my-heart 'yes.' It was an 'I-have-an-opportunity-I-can't-pass-up' kind of 'yes,' like I had to prove my connection with Claire to these other women as a means to validate myself.

Claire walked up to me and asked, in all her frankness (that I would come to love but didn't at that particular moment), "Do you know me well enough to introduce me, Stacey?"

Oh, how could she? How mortifying!

I scanned her face as she smiled playfully with the question, steady in her gaze. I couldn't even answer, and she handed me a blue sheet with her bio on it. The words swam in front of me as I went into fight-or-flight mode. I had to perform. I had to get this right. When I stood up, I made an ass out of myself, saying things that drew more attention to me and didn't highlight enough about her. I may have impressed those women with my connection to Claire, but I felt empty inside. I had a relationship *to* Claire but was not yet in a relationship *with* Claire.

Why did I need to pretend to know something, or someone, when I didn't?

I do that with you, God, don't I? I act like I know you when I give women those formulas. But I haven't known you, at least not in a long time. I've kept what I thought was a safe distance from you because I've been afraid. It's easier to talk about you, especially to a room full of women who are afraid of you too. And like me for so very long, they don't even realize they are afraid.

In the space on the dock, these words came to me:

It's arrogance.

I drew the Spring air sharply into my lungs. Then blew it all out.

Oh God... it is. It's arrogance. You're right.

But I heard the revelation in a gentle way, in a way that wasn't trying to hurt me.

I've been so arrogant, pretending that I knew things I didn't really know. I've been so arrogant, introducing you to women when I don't even know you well enough myself. Just like I did with Claire. Trying to validate me while I was also trying to introduce you.

It wasn't exactly that black and white. I had genuine encounters with God, a genuine faith, and genuine desires to share that. But somewhere along the way, it got messy and I got stuck.

I took the pebbles from the grooves in the dock, throwing a handful into the water where they landed in a scattered rhythm. I did it over and over again until it became its own meditation. There was something soothing about the action.

God, I've been afraid to admit when I didn't know something. I felt so, so insecure, like I had to prove my worth through what I knew.

A feeling of recognition swept over me, not in the form of sadness, though. It was more of an understanding.

I'm sorry...

I said it both to God and to me.

The arrogance was a cover-up for my insecurity. I had never seen it before that moment.

To know the truth brought an ache but not a wound. Something inside of me felt freer to know this ugly and honest truth about myself. Funny, it didn't even seem ugly when it faced me, in the same way when they hand you your baby right after birth and it's covered with slime and goo with a squinched up, swollen face after squeezing and surviving its way through your birth canal. It's yours, and you're in awe of the miracle in front of you and the labor you endured to bring it forth. No matter what anyone else might think, your little messy miracle is beautiful.

The birth of this 'aha!' moment had a beautiful freedom to it. It seemed reasonable, actually… reasonable that I had used arrogance as an overcompensating mechanism to cover up the deep insecurity I felt with God.

It was new for me to hear the truth about myself and not reject myself for it and look away in shame. Instead of feeling like a failure and wanting to hide, I had compassion for myself.

My body relaxed even more as I exhaled.

The sigh felt like it was coming from that deep place inside of me – that spiritual place that felt liberated from a sort of prison. It was cathartic to know this and to see it for what it was… and to feel love for myself in the face of the failure I saw.

I found myself wanting to get on my knees and cast more pebbles into the rolling Hudson. The truth was sacred, and the dock had become my sanctuary.

And this God? He was more gracious than I thought He was.

"Stasha? Molly's here to see you." Rock was calling from the front while the boys were doing laps in the hallway.

"Out here, Mol... in the back!" I was so glad to see my friend was here. She and Paul had just told us they were moving down South at the end of the month. Paul was being transferred down to teach at University where a professor had unexpectedly passed away. My heart was nearly broken, as she was the one, true friend I sought out each Sunday to feel anchored to sanity. She was the only one on the board who knew what a labor it was to deal with Kathryn when she was at her worst, and she was one of the only people I could talk to about it all without feeling like I was a horrible person. There were only two weeks left of my sabbatical, and by the time I re-entered the position, Molly would be gone.

"Stace-a-roo!" Molly greeted me with a big smile and some Spring lilacs. I had never had so many nicknames as when I came back to the East Coast.

"Mol, you don't always have to bring me something," I told her.

"Oh yes, I do. I would have brought you a puppy if your husband would have let me," she plopped down next to me and put her feet on the wicker ottoman. Her ease with herself and me... her dry wit – I was going to miss her something fierce.

"Molly, you bring one of your new puppies over here and I'm going to stop being your friend. The last thing I need is something else to take care of. They're going with *you* to Virginia. Now get over it." She laughed and took some almonds out of her pocket to count. I rolled my eyes and smiled.

"Oh, don't you look at me like that. You know that 10 a day are good for your heart," she said. I was just waiting for the rest of the spiel. "And flax seeds, every day, will help you poop."

And there you go.

What is it with women in their 50s who have to talk about hot flashes and the power of fiber? I feared I was staring at my future.

"Okay, well, here's the latest..." Molly began. I sat up, ready for her to give me the weekly report of the board meeting. "We're getting some new window shades for the basement."

"Window shades? Mol, the basement is so freakin' dark. I think we need to get some more windows first," I chuckled.

She rolled her eyes. "Please. I can't believe I show up to vote on these things. Anyway..." She swallowed and took a sip of water that Rock had placed on the table beside her, sat back, and smiled in a pinched way.

"What?" I asked. It didn't look like good news.

"Stace-honey, I'm sorry. Kathryn has crossed the line. She met with the bishop for lunch last week and basically lambasted you," she said.

"Again? What? Why?"

Molly shook her head again. "You know Kathryn... she said you were housing some kind of evil spirit that was causing you to question your faith, and therefore, being rebellious.

It prompted her to hold a special ritual to 'clear the church.' She requested a special cleansing service be performed before you return."

I was dumbfounded. In Kathryn's mind, my theological questions were equal to insubordination. I knew that already. But my spiritual hunger for a real understanding of God was evidence of an evil spirit in Kathryn's eyes?

"Molly," I leaned forward, "please tell me that everyone was shocked." She just fixed her gaze on me and then softened it a bit.

"Honey, they weren't."

I shook my head again.

"They agreed with her?" I asked incredulously.

"Stacey, want to hear what she's done? She invited each one of them over for a special dinner and filled their ears about you. They have never been invited to social engagements with her before because she can't stand them – they are *beneath* her – but now that it serves her, well, you know…"

I looked out past Molly to the trees and breathed deeply. I couldn't take my eyes off of the swaying giants in my yard. I could sense there was more.

"What else, Mol? There's something else…"

Molly took another sip of water and put the glass down slowly, "She called a meeting with the local pastors in town for a prayer meeting for the village and felt that they needed to know of your friendship with The New Disciples, as well as your faith questions. Kathryn suggested that you were not fit to lead the music at the inter-faith conference next month and, after her presentation, the pastors agreed," Molly said.

"Really..." It was more of a statement than a question. "Nice. Really nice, Kathryn..." I shook my head, not even knowing how to respond.

I took one more breath before looking into Molly's eyes. I'd been working on coordinating the six other churches and music teams for the interfaith conference for months.

When I arrived in town, I'd worked to establish strong connections and my reputation with all of the denominations by attending their meetings and providing music for their special events. A bunch of the other music teams got excited about the idea of working together for a special interfaith concert, which had to be okayed by every presiding senior minister, which took a few more months of red tape and meetings. But it happened. The Catholics and the Baptists were going to work together for the first time in this little village. The Episcopalians and Seventh Day Adventists were going to join with the Presbyterians and Four Square congregants, and we were going to host it all in the backyard of the Methodist Church. It was almost a year of work and building credibility and vision, only to have it shattered in one short meeting.

"Honey, I'm sorry. I am so sorry. I didn't want you to hear it from her first. I wanted you to hear it from someone who loves you. I love you, Stace. Paul and I believe in you so much. I'm just so sorry," Molly lowered her eyes to her hand she had placed on my knee to comfort me.

The lump in my throat was too big, and words wouldn't come. I reached out to grab Molly's hand and turned my gaze back to the spruce trees, grateful that it was my friend who saw my hurt reaction...

And not my enemy.

19

The Gift of Judgment

"You can't wipe the pimple off the mirror."

Unknown

"Oh, Stacey! I finally got you!" It was Julie's sweet voice all the way from California.

"It's Julie," I mouthed to Rock, who walked into the dining room to see who had called. He gave me a thumbs-up.

"Julie. My friend. How are you and all those boys of yours? And how is your mom?" I asked.

"Oh, you know, Stacey… crazy as ever. The boys are all in a sport and have started their own band. We either have a basketball bouncing all weekend in the driveway or the drums and everything else playing after homework at night. It's a wonder I'm not completely insane with all the noise. I'm ready to come out there to New York and live next door to you for some peace and quiet."

"Funny, Jules," I couldn't help but smile. Her life was a circus in the very best sense, and I could picture her eyes widening as the ball was bouncing and the drums were playing. It was so nice to hear my friend's voice and to catch a glimpse of her life.

"And you know Agnes — she's running circles around all of us, as usual." We laughed. The woman had more energy in her 80s than all of us put together. Julie continued. "Now Stacey, tell me, what has been going on over there? Rocky filled me in a little when you were so sick. Are you better? And what about this crazy lady you're working with?"

Sighing, I found myself quiet for a moment. I took a deep breath.

"Jules, I'm not even sure where to start… "

But after a few minutes of bumping back and forth, I settled into the story about God's message to rest and all that had ensued with my doubting God and running headfirst into the brick wall of Kathryn. After about 40 minutes of sharing, I exhaled. "And that's basically it, in a nutshell." It was so quiet on the phone that I thought I had lost the connection. "Jules, you there?" I asked.

"Oh, Stacey. I'm here… I'm just taking it all in," Julie said.

"Okay, well, when you're done, would you tell me what you think?" I asked her.

There was silence as she pondered, "Stacey… first of all, I love you so much. I'm so sorry this has been so hard. I had no idea you were going through all this. Who knew that a trip out to New York was going to be well… such a *trip*?"

I rolled my eyes and sighed in agreement. *Who knew, indeed.*

"Thanks, Jules. I know… *I know.*"

We were both quiet.

"Stacey, do you remember a few months before you had Seth, you gave a talk for our women's group? You said something about how we treat people according to how we judge them. Do you remember that?" Julie asked.

"I remember that part, but I don't remember the whole gist of it. I was probably having baby brain."

"Well, I don't remember the whole thing either, but I do remember those words about judgment standing out to me, because it made me think about me and a friend from my Bible study. I had some soul-searching to do after you shared that, and I realized that I had been judging her."

Julie paused, and I let her words sink in.

"Stacey, do you think she's already judged you?"

"Yeah, she's judged me to be some insubordinate, evil-spirit-hotel of a human being," I said. It was quiet again, but I could picture Julie with her finger bent over her mouth like it usually was when she was thinking.

"Stacey, I know this woman has been a nightmare. Really. I mean, for how she accuses everyone of having 'this spirit' or 'that spirit', she sounds like she needs an exorcism herself."

I laughed.

"But Stacey, I'm wondering if maybe there is something you can talk to God about, too… maybe about how you might be judging Kathryn."

Man, oh, man…

I did not see that one coming.

If this had been another time in my life, I would have been so defensive. But when Julie threw it out there, I didn't feel angry or rush in to prove her wrong. She was so gentle and non-accusatory about it. I knew she loved me and she would never say something with the intent to hurt me.

"Julie, thanks. I mean it… I appreciate you saying a hard thing. I'll talk to God about it. It sounds like something worth considering." She exhaled and I could hear the relief in her breath. She was such a gentle soul, it probably stressed her out just to bring it up. "You're such a good friend, Julie-Babooli. What would I do without you?"

"Oh Stacey! I feel the same way. I've missed you so much. Look, I gotta pick up the twins from school. Can we touch base soon?"

"Of course! You go and tell them all 'hi' from me."

We said our goodbyes and I set the phone down on the dining room table, thinking about what Julie had said. The big window by the front of the house was beautiful and inspired me to enjoy the neighborhood view. There was Ed on the ladder, fixing the flood light, with Freckles the Wonder Dog circling protectively underneath.

Hmmmm… it looked like a parable for my life.

No matter how many times Freckles paced anxiously around the ladder, he couldn't protect Ed from falling. It was just wasted, nervous energy. If Ed was gonna fall, he was gonna fall. No amount of circling was going to change that.

It made me think about what Julie said – about examining my judgment for Kathryn.

It would be easier to avoid the subject altogether – to avoid seeing something ugly in me. I mean why should I put myself under a microscope when Kathryn was the obvious bad guy here?

But something wasn't sitting right with me…

I could waste my energy focusing on her failings, but that wouldn't mean that I wasn't judging her the same way I was certain she was judging me.

And that's what I needed to look at.

Because circling around the subject of what she did wrong wasn't going to help me any more than Freckles circling around Ed was gonna keep him from falling to the ground.

I was either judging Kathryn or I wasn't.

I needed to see the truth about me so that I could be free, regardless of what Kathryn was doing.

But I didn't even know what judgment was anymore.

I only knew what my experience had taught me.

My church experience told me that if you weren't a Christian, God had already judged you and was going to send you to hell.

That married people were judged as 'better' and 'more complete' than single people.

That Christians were allowed to judge Catholics as not being Christians.

The list is long and controversial within the church, between different denominations, and between different religions.

But it wasn't just the church where judgment showed up, it was the outside world too:

Some people judged Democrats as liberal, socialist idiots who were without a moral center.

While others judged Republicans as rich, uncaring snobs trying to keep the poor from being helped.

Celebrities and athletes were judged as 'gods.'

Men were judged as more valuable to employ than women.

School football programs were judged more worthy of support than music programs.

Thin people were judged more important than fat people.

And it just never stops.

Judgment is all over.

But isn't there a good kind of judgment and a bad kind?

I mean, if my neighbor is a pedophile, I wouldn't have him babysitting my kids – that's a form of judgment, right? I judge him as not safe, and I'm totally okay with that.

I judge fire as too hot to touch. *That's right, isn't it?*

Kathryn was doing the meanest and strangest things. How was I even going to see what part was an okay judgment and what wasn't? And how was I going to see what part was mine in the whole mess of it, when she was so distracting with her own part.

Rock used to say to me, "Sometimes it's hard to take our eyes off of someone who pours gasoline all over their body and lights themselves on fire."

Kathryn was in flames by her own doing, how am I going to figure out which part of me was burning her when she had created such a heated environment?

It sounded like I was going to have to do some kind of spiritual surgery to dissect one part from the other.

Hmmm…

God, would You show me what judgment is? Can you help me to understand it the way You want me to?

I looked out at that crazy dog one more time before I realized the sun was setting.

"I'm going to cook dinner!" I called out to anyone who might be listening. "Don't fall over from the shock. It's okay. You'll recover."

Driving on the thruway in upstate New York was a surprisingly pleasant experience and completely different from Southern California freeways. Gone were the days of trying to read the sideways, bubble-lettered graffiti on the I-5 up to Los Angeles and dealing with speed demon du jour in his Porche Carrera who caused some 12-car pile-up right in the middle of the morning commute because apparently patience doesn't come with a 6-cylinder 325 horsepower engine.

No, it was different here. Instead of concrete walls lining the roads, there were trees, tall and full of Spring. There were creeks and bridges with occasional farmhouses dressed in unusual colors like periwinkle and mustard and tangerine. And there were so few cars on the road that most of the time you could allow your mind to wander at 60 miles an hour and it felt like a meditation instead of the Indy 500.

Today, the boys were running errands with me, and we were doing our weekly grocery shopping. They had fallen asleep by the time we entered the thruway heading north to Kingston. I peeked in the rearview mirror to find Seth with his head drooping forward and to the right, while Caleb had his head tilted back and his mouth wide open. Neither of them appeared very comfortable, but then again, they were still at the age where they were flexible enough to bite their own toenails and put their feet behind their ears, so who was I to judge what was comfortable or not?

That spontaneous question made me think of my phone conversation with Julie.

Ever since we had talked, the whole idea of judging continued to come up during my resting times. I hadn't had any 'aha!' moments yet, so I just asked again, "God, would you show me what judgment is?" And left it at that.

My mind began to wander on the long, peaceful drive and my imagination conjured up a scene: The two 'players' were the rainbow colored VW bus in front of me and a weather-beaten 1980s metal-gray Ford sedan on its left. They were beside each other as I watched them about four car-lengths ahead of me, when suddenly I saw in my mind's eye, the Ford turned hard to the right and sideswiped the van, sending it careening off the shoulder with a flat tire.

Instantly the imagination vanished, but I was left with three choices:

1. To make a judgment that the driver was a bad person.

2. To make a judgment that the person was a bad driver.

3. To make a judgment that the person made a bad driving maneuver.

Contemplating those options, it hit me that saying the driver was a 'bad person' seemed extreme. I didn't even know the person, so how could I say he was a 'bad person'?

Yet, I've made those judgments all the time. Haven't we all?

How many times on the road have we been cut off and started yelling, "You IDIOT!!!" while standing on the horn and waving our middle finger in the air like it was our national flag?

We don't even see that as judgment. We see that as normal.

And then, when we get around the person who cut us off, we shake our heads so they can see our visible disappointment. When we turn to see who it is we've just put in his or her place, we see how old, foreign, or female that person is. We all have our own biases, and those are the common defaults.

We really like being right about how wrong other people are.

That's judgment.

I had been in that situation in California just a few months before we left.

The shopping center parking lot was busy that day. My windows were open to let the beach breeze in, and I had a freshly made latte to take with me on my errands sans little boys. I was just about to break free of the traffic in front of Pain du Monde when a navy blue pickup backed out of a spot in front of me.

"Thank you very much," I said sarcastically as I balanced my latte between my legs and slammed on my brakes. *Classic*

California maneuver. Back out first, then check to see if anyone else in the universe might be there. Freeeek...

The truck started to edge forward, and I hit my gas pedal a little too aggressively to make the point that I wanted to actually be someplace other than a parking lot all afternoon. That's when the truck driver slammed on the brakes.

Are you kidding me? Really?

I did a quick glance down to find my latte had sloshed out of the mouth of the lid and onto my jeans.

Really...

I caught the view of a ponytail from her side view mirror. *What is she doing driving a pick-up truck if she doesn't actually know how to drive a pick-up truck?*

By the time I cleaned up the coffee, she was heading toward the exit.

Please already. Get me out of here.

But she did it again. She brought the truck to a dead stop with me right behind her. *I am going to pull that ponytail right out of her head.* I was tempted to swerve to the left and go out of the 'enter-only' section of the parking lot when she finally turned to the right out of the exit.

Thank you, God. Finally. Get me away from this woman.

Out of the corner of my eye, I watched her immediately pull over to the shoulder of Campus Drive, and something inside of me told me to check on her. I parked my car in front of hers and, in barely-controlled frustration, I walked up to her side of the truck. Before I even got there, I saw the little one – probably not more than two years old in his car seat behind her. When she turned to me, she was flushed with tears in the corner of her eyes.

"You okay?" I asked, "What's going on?"

"Oh my God... I'm sorry! I gave my son one of those round peppermint candies from the dry cleaners and pulled out of the spot and looked in my rearview mirror – he was turning red. I couldn't get him out of his car seat, so I started banging on his chest. Oh, my God... I thought he was fine, but when I took off again, I heard him choking again," she said.

I turned my eyes to her son, playing with his child's set of big, plastic keys he probably used to drive his mother off the edge of a cliff. Kids are resilient; he had already moved on and was none the wiser. His mother, on the other hand, was completely wrung out and looked like she needed a spa treatment and a stiff drink. I put my hand on her arm. She was shivering, even though the sun was clear and warm.

"You're gonna be okay." I patted her arm. "He's already fine. I swear, whatever hair these kids don't turn gray, they make us want to pull out." She smiled weakly, grateful for the comfort and some understanding. We waited a few minutes, chit-chatting and breathing until she was okay to drive off. When I got back in my car, there was no more frustration; it had been replaced by compassion and an understanding that more was going on than I could tell from where I had been sitting.

Caleb rustling in his seat behind me brought me out of the California memory and back to the NY Thruway and the sideswiping scenario I had just created.

The truth was that I didn't know if the driver of the old Ford who did the imaginary sideswiping had suffered a heart attack or was swerving to avoid hitting something or fell asleep after spending all night at his wife's hospital bedside.

Or he might have been drinking all night or just gotten out of bed with his best friend's wife.

The truth was that I didn't know. And to act like I did, when I didn't – and to slap some label on someone else – is a judgment. I didn't know the totality of his heart or his life circumstances, so I couldn't judge the totality of who he was as a person. All I could say with certainty was, "That was a dangerous driving maneuver."

Judgment, the bad kind, is about labeling the whole of someone on the small part that I know.

And the part that I know is limited and filtered through my perceptions. Just like with the lady in the pickup truck in California. I took what was happening and filtered it through my inconvenience and frustration, creating an entire story based on that instead of what was true.

It seems there are different types of judgment. Some that serve us and other people – and some that don't. One that gets us closer connected to ourselves and others – and one that doesn't.

There's an observational kind of judgment: This fruit is red; this fruit is green. I like potato chips; I don't like pretzels. December is colder than June – well, not in Australia – but definitely here in New York.

Those are observations – and also a form of judgment. This kind of judgment is more like identification and definition.

But the other kind – the extreme, snap judgment or bias that calls something absolutely right or absolutely wrong, about something that is negligible or negotiable – that's the kind of stuff where judgment doesn't work.

Like when we say, "People who eat red fruit are better than people who eat green fruit."

"Anyone who likes potato chips and not pretzels is a moron."

"Only stupid people live where they have winter for six months out of the year."

"All Christians are self-righteous. All Jews are stingy. All Muslims are terrorists."

When we say stuff like that, it's a 'labeling' kind of judgment that comes from an "I'm right and you're wrong" point of view that alienates people from each other. It doesn't work; it doesn't make for peaceful or beautiful living.

But we do it all the time.

I do it all the time.

So, God...

I paused and reigned my rampant imagination back to the point at hand.

Where am I judging Kathryn in a way that's not good for me? Or for her?

Shoot! I interrupted my own God-question for another one. *Why do I have to care about what's good for her? The woman is pure evil. She's psycho and what's worse, God, is that she does it in YOUR name and screws with people about who YOU are! Why do You let her do that?*

The whirr of the car engine was rhythmic and hypnotizing. It calmed me and helped me to breathe.

I felt like I needed to address another thing that was going on in my head.

God, I'm concerned about my motivation to figure this out. I don't want to be asking for Your perspective because I'm chasing after it in some striving way to perform for You. Like I've got to figure this out and fix it before Your patience runs out with me. But I don't want to resist seeing what it is either. I want to sincerely know, but I'm scared to know, and I'm scared it's going to piss You off and freak me out. Whatever You're going to show me about myself, would You help me to seek it and see it from a place of rest?

I let the unforced silence be there. I let God be that spiritual surgeon and relaxed into His capable hands as I had been doing more and more.

The thoughts came to me with ease.

I have been judging Kathyrn as some spiritual Cruella de Vil, haven't I? I can't even see anything good in her sometimes, God. I forget she's a wife and a mom. I forget she's a woman in a man's profession. I forget that she has her own stuff.

When I say she's 'pure evil' – I'm judging her. Just like she's judging me to have an evil spirit because she doesn't like my questions challenging her.

My mind kept toggling back and forth.

But she doesn't make it easy to have compassion. I feel like I have to protect myself from her, God. She's acting like such a jerk.

The word 'acting' stood out to me.

Oooh, hey... There's a difference, isn't there? There's a difference between her 'acting' like a jerk and 'being' a jerk, isn't there? She's acting in wretched ways, doing wretched things, but I've labeled her as 'wretched' all the way through, haven't I?

That's all I see when I see her.

But there's more to her than what I see, isn't there?

Oh, crap...

But God, it's easier... it's easier to judge her than to interact with her. If I interact with her, I've got to be in that moment with her – vulnerable and representing myself, not defending myself. But if I judge her? I get to call her a 'controlling bitch', slap that label on the file with her name on it, and tuck it away. Then, anytime I deal with her, I get to pull out that file and be in the relationship with the label.

Instead of her.

Judging her is safe.

It doesn't require my heart.

But I don't know how to both open my heart and protect it, God. I still need help. Maybe I need to work on my part, but I don't want to be foolish... if someone comes to rob your house and hit you over the head, you don't give them the keys to the door and a club to whack you with.

How do I not label her as a 'psycho' but still protect myself from the stuff she's doing that is, well... psycho?

How do I not judge her completely when I don't trust her at all?

I sighed deeply. I was doing that a lot lately, sighing when I was encountering a truthful, honest moment. I had just gotten comfortable being that honest with God about my trust issues with Him. I figured I could handle being honest about Kathryn with Him, too.

In the space – the grace – of that moment, more revelations opened up to me.

Oh, God... when I judge her, I don't have to take responsibility for my life and what I want. It's my easy-out to make her the bad guy. Okay, admittedly, she doesn't need a lot of help from me... but I get to be her victim. When I judge her as wrong, I judge myself as right. When I judge her as an oppressor, I judge myself as oppressed. And when I do that, I am making her the excuse – the reason for my distress. That means she's got more power over my life than I do.

Am I not okay with having my own power? Did I lose it all those years ago as a child and never learned how to live in it? Is this my time to learn?

So many questions.

That old scripture about not taking a splinter out of someone else's eye when you have a log in your own suddenly came alive to me.

I couldn't really put the tweezers in Kathryn's eye to remove the splinter when I was blinded by the log of judgment I had about her.

There's so much to this... so, so much.

I didn't just judge Kathryn. I judged myself as unworthy and reject-able. I judged Rock as Superman and deserving of a better/different wife. I judged my kids as deserving of a better/different mother. I judged God as an angry and punishing taskmaster. I was driving around life judging everyone through my select filters, thinking that I had the truth dialed in.

I glanced in the rearview mirror to my back seat where my two little boys slept in car seats, 3,000 miles away from that shopping center and that blue pickup truck. That woman in California wasn't a bad driver or a bad person; she was dealing with something that I had no idea about until I got close enough to truly see.

That woman could have been any one of us.

That woman was Kathryn.

That woman was me.

20

The Big Reveal

"It is more fun to talk with someone who doesn't use long, difficult words but rather short, easy words like, 'What about lunch?'"

A.A. Milne

"Whatcha doing?" Rock saw me sitting with my Bible at the kitchen table.

"Where are the kids?" I asked, not answering his question.

"Oh, you know… playing with sharp knives by electrical outlets."

I raised my eyebrows, "Not funny, Mr. Robbins. Try again."

"I walked them over to Marianne's so she could watch them for a few hours. I've got all these taxes and paperwork that have been piling up for months."

Marianne was new to our world. She had raised her own kids to full grown but still looked like a young woman in her twenties with her fit little body, short brown hair, and easy smile. She was chronically good-natured and ran an in-home playgroup that she'd had for 20 years. The boys loved playing with the other kids in her yard where mud and puppies prevailed.

"Nice." I glanced up from my keyboard and caught his eye. "I'm sorry. I know this has been a lot on you. Thank you for all you've been doing while I've been unofficially, and well, okay... officially melting down this last year."

"You think it's only been a year?" He really enjoys his own sense of humor.

"Again with the 'not funny'." I said.

"So, let me try this again," he paused for a moment to see if I was paying attention, "what are you doing?"

"Oh, sorry... I'm just processing this judgment thing that hit me. I realized I've been avoiding parts of the Bible – and even the Bible altogether – because of what other people have said about it."

He furrowed his brows, confused.

I shifted in my seat.

"You know when one of your friends criticizes someone you've never met – and it becomes your perception of that person? That's like how I've been viewing God, the Bible, and everything – with this filter that is someone else's. Only that someone else isn't always another person, sometimes it's an old version of me. So, after all this time of asking God to show me who He is, I'm getting some different information, which is changing my filters. I'm just taking a look at the Bible through this new lens – trying to not see it through someone else's ideas or my old ones. Right now, I'm reading Daniel."

I had avoided the book of Daniel like the plague because some people in my church past had loved to scare the poop out of me and others with all the talk of the 'end times' which Daniel apparently referred to. They would deliver news of wars, earthquakes, and nuclear holocausts, with a strange enthusiasm, and every fear button in me ended up being pushed.

"So, what are you finding out?" He grabbed a cup of coffee and sat across from me.

I told him the story that stood out to me, the one about Daniel's gift of interpreting dreams. "The king, Nebuchadnezzar, had a dream no one else could figure out, so Daniel came and broke it down for him:

The king had this amazing kingdom, and he had started off pretty humble and gave credit to God for his unbelievably good life and beautiful surroundings. But then, he lost it. He started this whole, 'Yo! I'm the man! I'm THE one who made this all happen' and was taking all the credit for himself.

Well, when he did that, Daniel told him he was going to lose his mind, lose his kingdom, and live like an animal in the forest for seven years. Then, after seven years, the king would have this whole 'aha!' moment, remember God, and give God the credit again. When that happened, Nebuchadnezzer would be restored back to his right mind and to his kingdom," I said.

Rock nodded, "Yeah. I remember that story. Bummer of a dream."

"Yeah, I know, right? Well, for me, I can't shake the pride-thing in it. As I was reading, it felt a lot like me..."

He held up his hand to stop me, "Whoa, Sta – I hardly think you're walking around taking all the credit for how great everything is."

I smiled at his sense of justice for me,

"No, Rock, that's just it... it's just the opposite: I'm walking around feeling like I've ruined everything. That I've screwed up this job here. That I've disappointed Kathryn and made her behave this way. That I'm making your life a mess. That I'm the worst mom in the world..."

He shook his head, "But, that's so far from the truth, hon. I don't see you that way, the kids don't see you that way, your friends don't see you that way..."

I affirmed what he was saying, "That's the point. I think that's the pride in sort of a reverse way. Instead of taking credit for all the good, like the king, I'm taking credit for all the bad. I think it's rooted in the same pride but just shows up differently. I haven't even been able to hear what the truth is about my life, or who I am – not from you, my friends, and not even God – because I'm so busy thinking I know best. That my perception about how bad I am is the final word on me.

I haven't been letting any other input or evidence in – that's where pride comes in...

When I read this passage, it's like I hear Pride's mantra saying: 'I know better than God.'

As a result, I've been carrying it all. All of the blame. *All of the blame*..."

My voice trailed away as Rock stared out the front window, thinking on it all. I followed his gaze. We both sat watching a squirrel have a field day running up the big tree in our front yard.

After a minute or so, Rock said, "You'd have to be kinda nuts to think you're responsible for everything going bad... to live under that pressure would make you crazy."

"Exactly." I took a deep breath. "Rock, that pride/insanity connection is what I see in Nebuchadnezzer's story, too. He was so busy thinking he was right, that he missed seeing all the evidence around him.

And I'm not only looking at the crazy lie of 'I've ruined everything because I'm such a terrible person', but I'm also examining the theologies that I've made fit into that crazy mindset:

'God is so good

But I'm so bad.'

'Jesus died for me

But I'm nothing but a worm.'

How could I ever apply those beliefs to my kid? 'Now, son, I'm so good, but you're evil; yes, you came from me, but I'm not evil, YOU'RE evil – and if you accept me, I will love you, but until then, I'll have to withhold my love and eventually punish you.'

Doesn't that just make you go 'huh??' I mean, Rock, could you ever imagine saying that to the boys?"

He shook his head, "Sta, I'd never do that. It hurts me to even think about it. No way."

"Right? So, how can God be good and make me in His likeness and image, and I end up bad? I don't understand the math. How can bad come from good?"

I wrapped my hands around my coffee mug while I kept processing out loud, "And the whole 'worm theology' – 'I'm nothing but a worm' stuff. I don't get it. Why would Jesus die for a worm? Why would I serve a god who would have his son die for nothing? I would never want to teach my child that my love was like that: 'I love you, but you're lucky that I do, because you're not really worth anything.' It's madness!

I was taught this stuff at church and in the side conversations with others, but I wasn't taught to think through it, to test it, to see if it even made sense. So, I've been trying to figure out how to have this genuine faith – which I do – but so many of the premises have made me feel crazy. And when I question it out loud, I get punished or rejected or treated like I'm some kind of heretic instead of a thoughtful person who's trying to make sense of it all."

Rock put his hand out toward me, and I reached for his as he tried to process it all. "This is good stuff, Sta... really good stuff, but man, it's a lot to think about. I think I've just been in 'go-mode'. I don't even really think about theology in this way. When I've seen you wrestle with yourself, I've always thought that it was how you were raised and that the things that happened to you did a number on you, but I guess I didn't see how the religious end of things twisted how you saw yourself, too."

"Mmm hmmm. I get what you mean. But I think they all worked together... the family stuff and the rape – especially the whole idea of keeping secrets and not getting help or asking questions – all of this supported a lot of crazy ideas of suffering in silence, and it all probably set me up to think that a punishing God made sense. So when the idea was presented to me, I accepted it instead of resisting it and running naked and screaming for the hills."

He laughed, "Nice picture, thanks for that. Hey, I don't mean to do a flyby on this heavy stuff, but I have one question before I get to work."

"Shoot," I said.

"So, you asked God to show you who He is... Any word on that yet?"

"No," I laughed a little and got up to stretch my legs, "but it's weird, I don't feel restless about it in the way I did before. It's like... hmmm..." I gave myself a second to think it through, "I feel a sort of peace just to figure out what He's not. He's not The Big Terrorist in the Sky like I thought He was."

I walked to the bay window, leaned my body onto the wall beside it, and put my hand on the glass.

"It's been like looking through a windshield in a car that's covered with dirt, dead bugs, and rain... I kept thinking the stuff on the windshield *was* the view. But that was the arrogance, judgment, and pride I was seeing. That wasn't God. That was just the mess in me that became my filter and changed the way I've seen me, life, and what I called 'God'. But in my resting times, God's been showing me so much. I can see the dirt and stuff for what it is. I can see it's not Him." I knew it was a lot to digest so, I broke it down further.

"The arrogance – it's about my insecurity. I act like a know-it-all when I feel exactly the opposite.

The judgment – it's about my need to feel in control. When things feel too loose, I find a place to judge myself or others because it makes me feel safe to order my world with a 'this is right' and 'this is wrong' measuring stick.

And the pride – well, I'm still sorting that out. But it seems to be about trust. When I trust myself and God, I can be in partnership and hold my life together. But when I don't trust, I'm trying to carry the weight of the world on my shoulders. Even though that's God's job, it's like pride is saying, 'I'll do the god-job', but it makes me feel crazy. It's too much of a burden for me or for anyone.

That's all the stuff I thought was God. I think I've just been trying to feel safe because I didn't have peace. Once I saw that it was my stuff on the windshield and not God, I was able to wipe it away and look for the real God. I'm open to knowing Him – or It – or whatever God is, in a new way now that I know He's not the freaky Santa-Zeus-policeman god or any of the other characters I thought He was. I want to hear who He is, but I don't feel that striving anymore like 'I have to know, or else!' I just feel peace."

Rock smiled and got up to be near me, "I've seen a new peace in you. I see it in the way you are with the kids and the house. I see that you're not fighting to rest anymore – you're taking time. You're not so hard on yourself. You're different, Stasha." He put his arms around my waist and held me close.

"Yeah. I'm not done, but I am different. And I'm not actually worried about being done anymore. What has been so natural for you, Rock, has been so difficult for me. I have spent years wishing I could be like you."

Rocky laughed and stepped back.

"Sta, even though I appreciate that, we both know that I make you crazy. Bills pile up, the taxes are late… the first 10 years of our marriage were really, *really* hard because I made them that way. I think in the painting of yourself as 'all bad', you've made me 'all good'. I haven't been. I hurt you a lot and contributed to the unsafety and mess. I'm not done either. I've got things I need to work on in myself, too. I've taken you for granted and I've taken advantage of you. You are the queen of being intentional, and you're a visionary. I need more of that, and I think we probably see things in our spouses that we want for ourselves."

"Thanks for saying that. You're right. Those years were so hard. So painful. And even in trying to paint you as the good guy, while you were doing really hurtful stuff, it messed with my head. Maybe it still does. I'll examine that. I'm sure that I will have to look at that with a different lens as I walk through this, but as for your chill qualities: the truth is I would rather have had peace all these years. It always seems like a much happier place being you than me," I confessed to my husband.

He glanced at the clock, "Yeah, you've been a real freakin' nightmare." He winked. "But you're my girl and I'm your guy and we're both moving in a healthier direction, hon. And I… I have one hour to get the taxes done. Ain't gonna happen, my friend." He imitated one of our favorite comedians, Paul Reiser's voice.

"Oh Rock! We haven't even talked about starting back up at the church. It's next week!"

"Yeah. Not today. Marianne has the kids again tomorrow, and we can talk then. It'll be fine, Sta. You don't have to figure it all out. Remember?" He motioned with his hands,

"Big God part, little Stacey part." He walked through the kitchen and down to the basement, leaving me alone with my coffee cup and deep thoughts. I sighed and out of the corner of my eye caught Ed and Freckles the Wonderdog heading out for their afternoon walk.

My head lay deeply into the pillow that night. The street was its usual quiet, and all I could hear was the occasional scrape of the chair from the basement while Rock worked on taxes late into the night.

It had been so many years of sleeplessness, but as I learned to rest in stillness during the day, I began to pull that into the night. I didn't mind the insomnia anymore. It was my rendezvous time with God when everyone else was asleep. Some nights, something like a cloud would seem to envelop me as it filled the room and my head lay heavy with surrender. One night, as I just simply breathed into the experience, I licked my lips and found they tasted distinctly of cloves and honey. In those awake times, I invited Him to be who He was and to bring me the rest that He knew I needed. It didn't always come in the form of sleep; it sometimes came in that hazy, half-awake state, and then other times it came in just breathing in the stars that I could see out of my windows.

Either way, I would rouse refreshed, like Something Greater than me had exchanged the insomnia I had brought, with the serenity He offered.

When I first moved to New York and started this whole resting thing, the silence unnerved me, but now it was rich with wonder and mystery. This night was filled with that, and I lay there in a serene and sincere state of gratitude.

Thank you, God, whoever You are, for showing me these things about me that I couldn't see. I can't believe I'm saying this, but I'm glad to know where I've been arrogant, proud, and judgmental. I thought it would kill me to know all that but, whoever You are, You showed me in a way that made me not afraid to see it. Thank you.

The sound of my breath, pulling in slowly and deeply, relaxed me even more. My body settled in for whatever the night would bring. And that's when I felt the words – voiceless, clear, words – penetrate the darkness of the room and fill me in the most complete way:

I Am Love.

I closed my eyes, and a knowing smile formed on my lips as I answered back in my mind:

Of course You are.

It made perfect sense.

But the voiceless Messenger wasn't done. Words continued speaking to my heart.

And you are Love.

I breathed in the beautiful truth.

Oooh yes...

I am Love.

I lay there, just taking it in.

I am Love.

I cherished the feeling of what this meant.

Not just 'loved'

But 'Love'...

'Loved' had its own wonder to it, but it was different. It was a receiving state that I could be in – or not be in.

Yes, I could be loved, but I could also be unloved.

What I sensed God revealing to me was different than that – and so much more than that.

That 'love' was my identity – the DNA from His spirit to mine. He made me from who He is, from the very core of His nature.

And in that, there was no opposite. It was who I am.

It wasn't about being deserving or worthy or special.

It wasn't that I had done everything right or nothing wrong.

Or believed in a certain way or not.

This was about being created...

From Love...

To live in Love.

This was my very nature,

My design,

And my destiny.

It couldn't be taken away

Because it was woven into the fabric of my being.

It was the mystery of God in me.

It was my identity.

Who I am.

But it wasn't just me. It was everyone. If I am made from Love, then so are you. We all are.That's who we are. All of us. Even when we forget with some horrible plague of Spiritual Amnesia.

Whether I like you or not.

Agree with you or not.

Accept you or not.

Whether we vote or pray or live the same.

You're love too...

We're not broken, needing to be fixed. Or lost needing to be found...no. We're miracles needing to be reminded of how truly marvelous we are.

I needed that reminder. That's what this whole thing was about.

Me forgetting who I was and being called to 'Be still and know...'

Oh Spirit... thank you.

What no man gave me, no man could take away.

This was something transcendent. A knowing, deep within.

My body completely relaxed as I felt a tear stream down my temple, landing on the pillow. I already had a peace in the space of not knowing who He was, but this was different.

This was a peace with something else...

Something more...

Something that filled me – yes, something that satisfied me.

Knowing this God of Love and knowing this about me – well, it *stilled* me.

And something, in that moment changed me forever.

"Sta..." Rock whispered, "Stacey..." he was gently shaking my arm.

"Mmmm? 'Vrything okay?" My voice was slurry and warm and I couldn't really open my eyes, but I could feel the warmth of the Spring morning all over my body. It was calling me back to sleep.

I felt Rock touch my forehead.

"Stacey, you okay? You *feel* fine. No fever."

"Hmmm... honey, I'm fine. What's wrong?" I started to sit up. He sounded concerned, but I couldn't figure out why.

"You're not exactly one for sleeping in – or sleeping at all, for that matter. The last time I had to wake you up, you were sick. But last night, you weren't pacing around as usual. I took the kids out for breakfast and dropped them off at Marianne's. When I came back, and you were still in bed, I got worried."

I blinked a few times as I remembered the details of the night before.

God is Love.

Love made me.

I am Love.

Then, I fell asleep.

For the first time in almost two years, other than when I was sick, I had slept through the night.

I smiled at my husband.

I would tell Rocky the whole story later, but for now, I pulled him close with the warmth of my cheek on his. I loved this man, and he loved me – and for the first time, in a really long time – or maybe forever, I could actually feel it.

21

Traveling Mercies

"Caged birds sing of freedom, free birds fly."

Thorolf Rafto

"You ready?" Rock asked me.

"I am." I nodded. He brought us each a cup of coffee since he was still the only one in the house who made a cup worth drinking.

"Okay. Well, the board will meet tonight for their weekly meeting. The Wednesday night service is covered tomorrow, and we'll meet with Kathryn on Thursday to get ready for our first Sunday back."

I nodded again.

Rock raised his eyebrows.

"You going to just sit there, Ms. Zen Woman, or are you actually going to say something?"

I shrugged my shoulders, "I'm not really sure what to say." I answered.

"Stacey, do you still want to stay at this church and do this music thing? Do you even want to deal with Kathryn and all this stuff?"

His questions were fair and frequently asked by both of us, but in light of all that happened and how much I had changed, they felt new.

"Rock, I have rarely placed the thought about church anywhere near the question of 'Do I want this?' I just felt like I should because I thought God would be happy – or happier – with me. That it was 'the right thing'. So, 'Do I want to?' is a new concept to me."

He understood. We had used phrases like "We feel led" or "We feel called" or "This is our purpose." And none of those words are bad or wrong, but they had been used to cover up things that we thought were less noble – or even sinful – like "I want" or "I'd like" or "This would make me happy." My desires were always second to 'my ministry'. Did I want to stay here and work with Kathryn? I didn't have the strength in those muscles yet, so I didn't know. I think I needed to talk to her.

So, without thinking twice about it, I picked up the phone.

"This is Reverend Kathryn."

"Hi Kathryn, It's Stacey," I began. My stomach fluttered a bit, but it didn't last long.

I could hear her huff a little. I still wasn't calling her "Reverend."

"Well, hello Stacey. Are you feeling well yet?" She asked with a hint of British accent creeping into her voice.

"Thanks. You know, I feel stronger every day and I'm still working on it. Ummm... I wondered if you'd like to join me on a walk this afternoon. It's going to be one of those perfect Spring days, and I thought we could catch up on a stroll over at the park, say around 2 o'clock... what do you think?" I asked, hoping against hope she would say yes.

Her guard was up, which I completely understood, but she agreed anyway. "Fine. I'll meet you at the gate by the police station."

"Perfect. Thanks, Kathryn. See you then." I breathed a sigh of relief.

It was when I hung up the phone that I realized I had no idea what I was going to say. But whatever it was, and whatever happened, it was all going to be all right.

The air had an almost buzzing quality to it. The sky was extra blue, and the clouds were a fluffier white. I couldn't tell if it was the contrast from the long winter of the North East that was making it seem that way or if this was the way Spring had always been.

Or maybe it was just me.

I saw Kathryn standing at the gate. She jutted out her neck and adjusted her collar. She seemed smaller to me, less imposing. I kissed her on the cheek and greeted her. It was our customary salutation, regardless of how we felt, and for once I didn't feel like one of us was playing the part of Judas.

"Hello, Kathryn," I said.

She began by making small talk, asking after Rocky and the boys as we walked along the outline of the large, square perimeter of the park. When we reached the bleachers, we sat and faced each other.

"Stacey, the board and I have been working very hard. In this last month that you've been gone, we have bonded in a new way." I resisted rolling my eyes, but I thought about it.

Yeah. I heard. At my expense…

"You know the problems they've had adjusting to me, and these more *structured, godly* ways that I've brought. They've never had that before. Well, they are ready to move forward with me and my vision. We are united."

She waited for my acknowledgment, but I simply met her eyes with mine, waiting for her to go on.

"You and Rocky are welcome to join us in our vision, but things will have to change. I will need you at the board meetings, showing your full support of me and the vision. You will be expected to come to the Bible study that I am holding, and you will need to do morning and evening prayer from your prayer book at home, holding our church and each member in it, in prayer. And we will be there for you, as family for you. We will be praying for you and helping you as you raise the boys and take your ministry further. We don't want you to just do the music anymore; we want to be bonded together – but we need your commitment to the church," she said.

I listened intently while she spoke. I had forgotten how pretty she was. She really was a striking woman.

The exhale of my breath was louder than either of us expected and it made me laugh a little. I was doing that more – laughing at myself instead of beating myself up.

Kathryn wasn't asking for anything unreasonable, and she was willing to make an exchange: my commitment for theirs. It was a fair deal for all intents and purposes.

"Kathryn, thank you for the offer. I know this is not only your career but also your spiritual mission and passion. And I want you to know that I never planned on coming out here to turn your world upside down. I really didn't. I came out here on the same page as you in many ways but... something has shifted for me. And while you may believe that it was something ungodly that was provoking me, what I see is that it was the goodness of God drawing me."

I paused for a moment to take a breath. "While I thought I was being called out here to do music with you, I now see that there was something more happening... something unraveling and unfolding at the same time. It's been unnerving to go through so many spiritual doubts and to have my faith – and my work -- be so affected. I didn't mean to go through this all on your watch. In fact, I never really saw it coming, if you can believe that."

Her shoulders relaxed, and her face softened slightly at my unexpected honesty.

I went on:

"The people in our church want someone who shares their way of seeing God and can celebrate that with them without reservation. I understand that's what you're asking for, and it's a totally reasonable and fair request."

I shifted and looked out at the vast nature around us, recentering as I took a deep breath. The trees were a strong presence surrounding the field. They seemed so brave and made me feel brave too.

I turned back to Kathryn, "You deserve to have what you are committed to, and I… well, I think I am ready to move on to whatever is next, even though I'm not quite sure where that will be."

I nodded at my own words and felt tears come to my eyes, allowing myself to feel the emotion, something I wouldn't describe as sadness, but there was an element of that to it. Mostly, it was just permission to feel what I couldn't explain and let the tears be my words when I had none to speak. If it had been last year, I would have held them back so as to not give her the upper hand. It was different now. I was different now. They were *my* tears for *my* feelings and *my* reasons. They were for *me*.

Kathryn sat taller. She seemed relieved but wanted to keep her business face on, "Well, we will need to work out the details according to our original agreement. You can complete your two weeks of music and then the board will meet regarding the rest of the details," she said, showing little emotion.

I nodded. It all sounded fine to me. They were ready to move on to what they were looking for, and I was ready to move on because of what I had found.

And just like that, it was over.

"Wow. So, what did you say after that?" Rock had waited all day until the kids were in bed to hear the whole story.

"Mmmm... let me think. I just let her cover the details, and I think that was it." I said.

"How did you end? I mean, how do you walk away from something as awkward as that?" he asked.

"You know, I just looked at her, Rock. I mean, *really* looked at her. I saw somebody who's got her own thing with God. She uses the collar to cover up her insecurity in the way I used my arrogance. She's got her own stuff. I don't really feel the need to figure her out. But, I'll tell you, I couldn't in good conscience agree to the terms, even though they were fair and just as they should be. I definitely know that I don't want to go back to that punishing type of God paradigm again... I just don't."

His head was affirming that for both of us as I went on.

"I'm going to say something that sounds crazy, and I'm not saying I don't have things to work on inside of me, but I truly felt love for her – love and understanding. I felt connected to her, not because we share the same faith but because the same Faith shares us. That God, who is Love, who made me, made her too. We are connected forever by that, even if we never see each other again." I felt a sense of release from just getting the words out.

"Well, Sta, you're a much better person than I am. I don't know if I'd be as gracious with all she put you through."

He shook his head, and I could see him replaying the craziness of the last year. I walked up to him, put my arms around his waist, and stared into his kind eyes.

"Rock, you and I both know I'm not a 'much better person than you.'" I smiled. "I'm a slightly better person than you."

We laughed. It felt good to laugh.

"Seriously, I'm just in a different place than I was." I assured both of us.

"I get it, Sta. You know, it's weird... now that I know you're all right, I'm starting to have feelings of wanting to strangle her. I think I held back because of how over the edge you were. But now, I've got my own thing to process through with this. I'm glad we were here. I don't like what we went through, but I do like what it produced in you. That is a gift in our family." I nodded. He was right, and we both knew it.

"And you know what else?" He pulled me near to his body.

"What, love?" I was pretty sure I knew the answer.

"I'm ready to go home," he said.

And so was I.

Gina made a carrot cake for our last Sunday at the church. The new yellow curtains were up in the basement, and people gathered around to say good-bye. It was a short affair, and while there were a few people who were genuinely sad to see us leave, there were others who we felt a mutual air of relief. They could move on in the direction they wanted and so could we. This was just a way of finishing well.

What needed to heal – our disappointing the congregation or Kathryn's demonizing us – was going to need to heal over time and with some distance. And with the God of Love doing what He could do and I couldn't.

Kathryn wanted to give a final blessing and stood beside Rocky. She always felt more comfortable around him since he was the more affable of the two of us. But she had no idea how irritated he was with her, and when she put her hand on his shoulder, I watched him stiffen. "Rocky, why don't you tell everyone about what the future holds for you," Kathryn invited him to share.

Rock cleared his throat and looked down for a moment. "Well, a friend of mine has an IT company back in California, and I'm going to work for him. I've got a natural ability for computers and a lot of years when my single mom worked for Boeing in electronics, but I've never done this before. It's a new start and one that we feel good about. Stacey is going to keep on with the boys at home, prepare to get them homeschooled in the next couple of years, teach some music lessons, and speak at a few women's retreats that she has coming up. We want to thank you and tell you that we bless you and will think of you often."

"And we, you: Rock, Stacey, Caleb, and Seth." Kathryn smiled toward the boys in that reserved, priestly way and invited everyone to join her in prayer. I didn't really hear what she was saying because I was busy looking at everyone while they prayed. I saw people bowing their heads, squinching their eyes, and some of the older men, looking like this was a fitting time for a nap. If anyone had opened their eyes and seen me staring back, it would have freaked them out, I'm sure. But this is what was comfortable for me... and I wasn't worried at all that this was breaking one of God's rules.

I just knew that I couldn't do my spirituality in this way anymore. It was time to be true to my heart and to this God who had revealed Himself to me.

"May you go forward to love and serve the Lord." Kathryn raised her right hand and made the sign of the cross in the air.

Rock squeezed my hand while we stood quietly until we all answered – and for a variety of very different reasons:

"Thanks be to God."

"Well, good morning, folks. This is your captain speaking." The warm syrupy, soft Texan drawl mixed with just the right amount of authority grabbed my attention.

"It looks like we are number seven in line once the fog lifts, so just settle on back and relax. We'll be in the air in no time. Your safety is our first priority. Thank you for flying Continental."

The crackly speaker switched off, and I unbuckled my seatbelt, shifting in my bulkhead seat. *Hmmm, yeah. This could take a while,* I thought.

In the world of airlines, time is relative, like the last two minutes of a football game. Twenty-five minutes later, there is still one minute left to go.

I reached down and grabbed my laptop to catch up on some email. I waited for the computer to wake up when I noticed that my seatmate was already asleep, his mouth slightly gaping. *Good for you, I'm more relaxed than I used to be, but that whole 'going-to-sleep-before-take-off' is a real gift.*

We had been back in California for a year, and here I was, coincidentally, heading back to New York to speak at my friend's church in Manhattan. He was one of the few who welcomed the new me back into my old world. It seemed that my simplified message of a God of Love wasn't sitting well with some of my friends or some of the churches I used to go to where they had hired me to speak and sing.

Not enough rules inside of me and too much wiggle room to mess up, they said.

Too much freedom.

It made people uncomfortable.

They wondered if I was a loose cannon or a modern-day hippie who was going to lead people away from Jesus and down some strange path of destruction.

It took me a while and some tearful soul-aches to realize that I could not convince people that my new way of seeing life was a good/God thing. I didn't even have a need to convince them. That had gone away, too. I invited them to come into my world and see for themselves, to ask me any questions they wanted – but even when they *did* venture close enough to take a look at me, my life, and my peace, it didn't guarantee that they would see past their own judgments.

But being someone who loves being around people so much and finally being healed enough to truly be *with* them in beautiful ways without those old filters and coping mechanisms, it became a deep grief to not have my community to share this joy and freedom with. And so I mourned the death of the old life, friends, ministry, work, and community that, literally, had been my world.

People were afraid of my version of God.

But I was finally at peace.

God's gift to everyone. Peace. No special country-club handshake required. No jumping through wild spiritual hoops that were on fire. Nope. This seemed to me, an unconditional, no-strings-attached, *'No really, I mean it'* kind of peace.

A God of Love introduced Himself to me in New York, and that same God was my companion and comfort during the adjustment period back in California. The driving need to be on a stage, fueled by the unhealthy parts of me that wanted attention and accolades, had gone away. A deep, genuine desire to bring a meal to a pregnant neighbor, or a bag of groceries to the local school for a family in need, or to sit with a homeless man who I would have normally avoided, rose to the surface of my life.

Because I was back in the thick of everything familiar, life was confronting me at almost every turn,

Upstate New York had been filled with many trees and not so many people. It was simpler to be undistracted with God in this deep unraveling of my spirituality when there was nothing much else around, in the same way that it's easier to focus on your new husband when you're on your honeymoon.

But being back in SoCal with this new love for God was like returning back to 'real life' and trying to figure out how to integrate it all together after the honeymoon. Now was the time for the 'marriage' and next steps and deepening of that trust that would be tested in different ways in familiar surroundings – tempted to get busy, to get into needless routines, tempted to default to friendships instead of cultivating the intimacy of alone time with God.

So, the rejection I experienced from others became strangely holy – albeit, heart-breaking – bringing me back to the place inside where that peace lived. Forgiving. Understanding. Accepting.

God was always there with me before New York, threaded through my wildly accurate intuition, musical gifts, strange ideas, misperceptions and pain. He beckoned me to open my eyes and see that there was something more than the version I was settling for but couldn't sustain.

Something *love*.

And it satisfied me.

So, I was able to feel:

Peace and pain.

Peace and sadness.

Peace and frustration.

Peace and the seeming injustice.

Before New York, if I had felt that I had disappointed someone or been misjudged or failed them in some way, my peace would leave. Now, it was anchored *in* me. *With* me. *For* me.

It wasn't a perfect process; it was an unfolding one.

I looked out the window to see the blue sky where the foggy clouds had canvassed the runway. My eyes lowered to the sea of buildings lining the perimeter to my left.

Suddenly I saw the word... *that* word, on the top of one of the buildings.

I had taken off from John Wayne Airport so many times, but I had never noticed it before.

There it was – clearer – as the fog lifted completely.

Stillen

For anyone else, it would have just been the name of a company on an unremarkable office building, but for me, it was like a homecoming – bringing back a flood of memories that warmed me and reminded me of all that I had lived through, and all that now lived in me. I shut my computer and closed my eyes, leaning back into the memory of all that God had done by simply drawing me to do one thing: to rest.

I sighed and started to drift off when I felt the hand of the flight attendant touch my shoulder.

"Ma'am? We are being cleared for take-off so it's time to buckle up. It's going to be a great trip, but it's going to be a little bumpy starting off," she said kindly as she moved on to the passengers behind me.

I smiled and nodded. She was more right than she realized.

I knew from experience that some of life's greatest adventures started off

just

that

way.

"A man with an experience of God

is never at the mercy of a man with an argument."

Leonard Ravenhill

Join me in the conversation:

www.staceyrobbins.com

Instagram: @lovestaceyrobbins

Facebook: Stacey Robbins

Pinterest: @lovestaceyrobbins

GRATITUDES

Normally, I start a book with the gratitudes, but this time – this book – I wanted it to be like the last bite of the meal that you strategically set aside because it's your favorite and you want to be left with this yumminess in your mouth for as long as you can.

These people are my favorite flavors...

Rock: My husband, who calls me the 'Lucy' to his 'Ricky' – it's not been easy to grow and, thereby, call each other to grow – *I get that.* There is no one I'd rather grow with than you. Spiritually, you were so unencumbered when I met you and then, I dragged you into the mess of my complicated beliefs. Then, when I walked away from it all, you were left holding the bag in that, "Wait. What?" kind of way. Thank you for always being willing to support my process and never being intimidated by my next steps. Thank you for celebrating me with curiosity while you held your own space to be freely yourself. That is a rare and beautiful gift and I am grateful.

Caleb and Seth: I love being your MamaLlama. Best job in the world. I believe you both drew Dad and me toward these adventures that unraveled our faith because your souls called for freedom. How generous of you enter the world through our messy love, and to invite us into a healing and liberty that matched your own. You've taught me more about life, love, and God than anyone in my life. You call me on my shit with 100% commitment to me. Your love is safe for me to be my right-now self and my future-becoming-better self. You've taught me that I can be both eternally *who* I am and humanly *where* I am at the same time and be loved for all of it. I'm honored to be your Mom and to have you re-teach me what love and family are through your generous, gracious, and committed ways. If God gave me a magic wand to change anything about you, I would roll my eyes and point the damn thing at my hips because you both are more than I could have dreamed.

Heroes of God Loves Me, I Think...

Darin Hufford: You told me in 2009, "You need to write a book." I said, "I really don't. I'm good." And then, you know... this happened. You were one of the first people to open your arms, your family, your podcast mic, your publishing connections, and your community to me when many in the church closed their doors on me. You and Angie and the kids showed me that Jesus and fried food can heal an outcast's heart. Thank you for letting me in and having your love, humor, and truth surround me in a way that made me feel God. You are one of the most interesting chapters in my life story and I will never forget you or stop being grateful for you. Love you, D. Thank you for being you and letting me be me.

Ken Tamplin: Family. Friend. Trusted Advisor. Brother. When some of the church leaders told you to walk away from me when they didn't understand my newfound peace and deeper/lighter faith, thank you for standing close and staying true. I am grateful for your fierce love and protection and that you declared yourself my "Bill W." – which I had to look up – and when I did, it made me smile and feel like I would never be truly alone as long as you were in the world.

Nigel Skeet: The title of this book and my life wouldn't be the same without meeting you through our dear friend, Ken. Our conversations saved me during those crazy, insomnia-filled nights, texting on flip phones from New York to Los Angeles. And then, there was the truck driving back from New York…

David Trotter: Book cover photo, dream weaver, 'You've got this, Stace!' cheerleader and dear friend. So grateful for your relentless belief in me and your mad skills that make almost no sense to me that they all can reside in one person. Maybe that's why you're so tall…you needed a lot of room for all that magic.

Brad Cummings, Wayne Jacobsen, & Mick Silva: Thank you for being an important part of my story getting some legs to it as it toddled around like a drunken monkey in the beginning stages of its development. Your unique approach to sharing the God-stories of others out in the world has made a difference in the spiritual conversation. I appreciate you and your families, and I bless you for taking the beginning steps with me so many years ago.

Jessi Bass: What you get when you smoosh a spiritual daughter, dear friend, mentee, personal inspiration, trusted confidante, sprite, and psychic assistant all together in one. And who made me an "Aunt Stacey" to Eli Beli and Jamie Jamerson – which is one of the best line items in my Life Resume. Thank you for seeing me and believing in me. I love you, Hess. You're one of my favorite typos.

My editing team of dear friends: You're the safest people to see my faults. Thank you for catching all the misprints and mistakes and making the bigger vision the main focus. That's how you treat me in our friendship when you see my gaffes and I love you for it: *Lisa Espinoza, Tracy Panzarella, Irene Dunlap, Carissa Boles* (how big was the truck filled with our stuff that you drove from SoCal to Upstate??? THANK YOU!!! You are so damn brave), and *Gregg Farah*. With a special thanks to you, *Gregg*, for living through the realtime of so many of these events since we were teens. Your dedication to this book getting out there, will always have a special place in my heart and in this work in the world. Thank you, friend.

Always thankful for my steady and true friends: Angela Ippolito-Cottam & Dave Cottam, Beth Prizer (for doing that Shamanic work to release these pages back to me), Phil & Alicia Shinners, August & Hal Brice, Lance & Lyndia Leonard, Linda Masterson, Jeannine Janicke, Susannah Parrish, Carolee & Jeremy Dalton, Chris & Sarah Scott, Ralph & Laurie Umbriaco.

Great supporters and champions for my spiritual journey and the work of this book: Julie & Rick Sherburne, Tricia & Lee Heins, Mary & Reagan Lee, LoriBeth Auldridge, Josh Reeves, Anna Boneh, Tom & Hollyse Cooper, Jon Uhler.

And special thanks to our cover models, The Willis Family: You will forever be one of my favorite Sidecar Bakery memories! Thank you to *Travis, Courtney, Bodie and Walker* for playing the younger version of us. We are grateful to know your beautiful family and thank you for gracing the cover of this book!

This is going to sound weird but I truly mean it: For all the people who were part of my pain and my process – who forced me to look deeper and not settle for less than Love – the messy, judgmental, and rejecting people – especially in the name of God... *I am grateful for you.*

I learned how to use what happened, to become who I am and to help others to re-become who they are after their pain caused detours and spiritual amnesia. It is my honor to know I have the power to transmute hard things into love and to show others, just like me, the Alchemist power that lives inside all of us.

I wouldn't wish what happened to me on anyone. And yet, I am grateful that I have healed to better ideas of life, love, and God through it all.

And of course, my deep, deep gratitude to the messenger of the Messenger, who showed up in Harrisburg, Pennsylvania. In a town I hadn't planned on stopping in, a hotel I hadn't planned on staying in, and a lobby breakfast bar I hadn't planned on eating in. Thank you for being my loving, persistent, reminder to *"rest, dammit, rest"*: **Nancy Smith – a.k.a 'Nancy, from Alaska'.**

To the **Messenger, Founder, Creator, Source, and Sustainer of Love,** I am grateful for life and the opportunity to discover what it means to live in Love and live that out in the world.

My life is Yours.

Your life is mine.

We are all connected through the Divine thread of Your Love.

AUTHOR - TRUSTED ADVISOR - ITALIAN RETREAT GODDESS

Stacey Robbins is the award-winning author of *You're Not Crazy & You're Not Alone, An Unconventional Life: Where Messes and Magic Collide*, and *Bloom Beautiful*. Her writings are filled with gut-honesty and humor as she tattles on herself, sharing stories of marriage, parenting, health-issues, travel, and spirituality. In her recent offering, *God Loves Me, I Think... Stories from Hell, Heaven and the Other Side of Texas*, Stacey invites you on her spiritual journey as she travels cross-country, unraveling her ideas of life, love, and God as she moves from stuck places to free, anxious places to peace, and 'fear' places to love. Stacey lives between California, Texas, and Italy and is in love with her husband, Rock, and two sons, Caleb and Seth. www.staceyrobbins.com

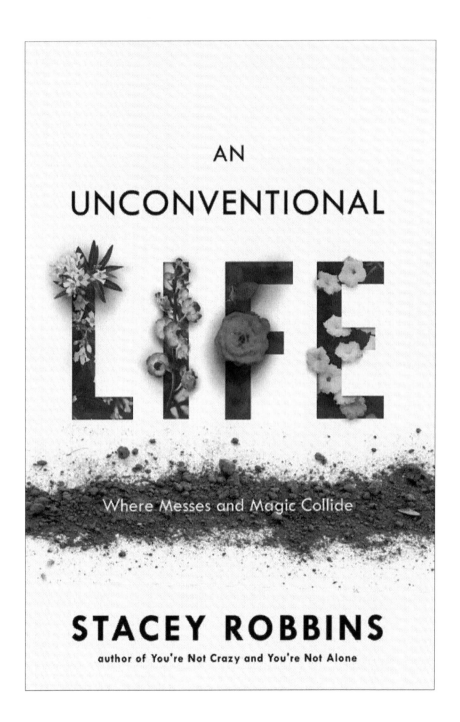

AN

UNCONVENTIONAL

LIFE

Where Messes and Magic Collide

STACEY ROBBINS

author of You're Not Crazy and You're Not Alone

You're Not Crazy & You're Not Alone

Losing the Victim,
Finding Your
Sense of Humor,
& Learning to Love
Yourself Through
Hashimoto's

STACEY ROBBINS

Bloom Beautiful

» life grows better when it's planted in love «

Inspirational musings and memes
by Stacey Robbins

MORE ADVANCED PRAISE FOR GOD LOVES ME, I THINK...

This is the account of the dismantling of one's faith at its finest: with no brutal, ugly, magical, or mystical part to spare. Sometimes to get to the Holy Land of a peaceful, clean space, you end up making a bigger mess to start with. The courage it took for Stacey to question the mess of beliefs she equated with Truth (what an existential risk!) on her journey to Peace, and the freedom it lead her to... can give even the most dissatisfied but scared-to-poke-the-beast seeker the courage to hear the message of this book. That God *is Love. The freedom you can glean from this truth and Stacey's journey has the power to deeply transform your pain into Peace.

Jessi Kristine
Artist, Certified Health Coach, and Doula

In the first pages of the book Stacey notes she is writing to you, the brave one. As I've pondered what that means I can't help but think that it's much easier to be brave when you have someone holding your hand and showing you the way. Stacey writes with such honesty and vulnerability, sharing her life's story in a fashion that invites you to feel safe with your own spiritual wonderings. As I was turning the pages it's as if I was right there, traveling along with her as she discovered she could trust that God is in and around and through it all. What an encouragement for the restless soul to be at ease. To trust that God is with you right here and now, wherever you are on your journey.

Alicia Shinners
Mama of 3, Postpartum Doula, INHC

Sure, on the surface this book is full of stories that are incredibly fun, relatable and enjoyable. Stacey is a captivating and emotional writer, and you will relate with these stories on a very human level. They feel true to the messy and sometimes painful experience of life we find ourselves in.

But there's something more. Beneath the stories, you will feel the longing for purpose and meaning, that is also part of this human experience. If you allow it, you will feel your own soul stirring in these pages. And, along with the author, you may find a little more peace for the journey as well. Enjoy!

Phil Shinners
Former Pastor, Spiritual Explorer and Guide, & Craft Beer Enthusiast

God Loves Me, I Think is the book you must read if you have encountered any doubts, questions, or obstacles in your spiritual or faith journey. And while this book contains both questions and answers, you will not find either in the expected form. Rather, this book is about what one person discovered about her own belief in God and God's belief in her.

But God Loves Me, I Think is not an exercise in self-indulgence. It is a straightforward, honest catharsis that is for anyone who is examining their faith... written with a sincere effort to help others realize that our faith journey, with all its warts and wrinkles, is sometimes an ugly process, and Stacey Robbins give us hers with all its stinky diapers, snotty faces, and even cellulite which she relates with wit and her self-deprecating sense of humor that at times reminded me of Shirley Jackson's Raising Demons.

And so, *God Loves Me, I Think* is not the usual drivel we find in tomes of this genre. On the contrary, this author strips herself bare in a compelling narrative of self-disclosure that invites the reader to feel safe about our own questions and doubts.

It is not a "how to do it" book—Stacey Robbins never preaches or lectures us about what we must do or how to go about it. Instead, she narrates her own travels through a difficult faith journey. Many of us have more than one faith journey during which our most essential beliefs and values are tested and challenged. The quintessential question is not merely how we meet the challenge or even whether we pass the test, but how we go about it and what we learn from the process. We are admonished to seek the "better angels of our nature"; however, those "angels" are both intrinsic and extrinsic. They are not only within us, but they are also around us in those persons who guide us and even help change our direction. Stacey Robbins tells us how she was guided by such angels.

Regardless of your religious beliefs or whether you are religious at all, *God Loves Me, I Think* is an important book if for no other reason than what is revealed to Stacey Robbins at its climax, which you will have to read to discover yourself. But Stacey Robbins faith journey transcends the existential elements of religion and belief to a higher level of life, its meaning and purpose. *God Loves Me, I Think is* a compelling confession of what Stacey Robbins encountered in her transition from roving to "rest."

Thomas H. Cooper
Professor of Sociology

Do you believe in a mean, scary God but are trying to be a peaceful, loving person? *This book is for you.*
Hurt by 'church people'?
This book is for you.
Have questions and doubts, but are scared to ask them or even think them?
This book is for you.

God Loves Me, I Think is a compelling journey of a faith unraveling in the most essential ways... written by one of the good ones. Stacey's been where some of us are too afraid to go, but through her brave journey, she's found a peace that many of us long for.

If you're seeking a God of Love, a God of Peace, a God who will be with you in all the twists and turns of doubt until you find your way back home to Love again... *this book is definitely for you.*

Carissa Boles
Foster Child Advocate and Recovering Church-a-holic

Made in the USA
Middletown, DE
19 October 2022

13054361R00148